# THE RESPONSIBILITY OF INTELLECTUALS IN THE AGE OF FASCISM AND GENOCIDE

BOSTON REVIEW



*The Responsibility of Intellectuals in the Age of Fascism and Genocide* is *Boston Review* issue 2025.3 (Forum 35 / 50.3 under former designation system).

Printed and bound in the United States by Sheridan.

Distributed by Haymarket Books (www.haymarketbooks.org) to the trade in the U.S. through Consortium Book Sales and Distribution (www.cbsd.com) and internationally through Ingram Publisher Services International (www.ingramcontent.com).

Image on pages 6 and 7: Getty Images

To become a member,
visit bostonreview.net/memberships.

For questions about donations and major gifts,contact Jasmine Parmley at jasmine@bostonreview.net.

For questions about memberships, email members@bostonreview.net.

Boston Review
PO Box 390568
Cambridge, MA 02139

ISSN: 0734-2306 / ISBN: 978-1-946511-97-3

CONTENTS | SUMMER 2025

**Editors' Note** 4

FORUM

**The Responsibility of Intellectuals in the Age of Fascism and Genocide** 6
*Robin D. G. Kelley*

**On the Responsibility of Historians** 26
*David Waldstreicher*

**On the Responsibility of Journalists** 30
*Jennifer Zacharia*

**On the Responsibility of Citizens** 35
*Martin O'Neill*

**The Mamdani Model** | COLUMN 40
*David Austin Walsh*

**Building a Political Home** | INTERVIEW 49
*Cathy J. Cohen with Brandon M. Terry*

**Gaza and the End of History** | ESSAY 66
*Joelle M. Abi-Rached*

**Celebrating 50 Years of *Boston Review*** 78
*Nathan J. Robinson on Noam Chomsky, Rick Perlstein on Elaine Scarry, Lea Ypi on Joseph H. Carens, Susan Faludi on Vivian Gornick, Ryu Spaeth on Merve Emre, Jay Caspian Kang on Olúfẹ́mi O. Táíwò, Naomi Klein on William Callison & Quinn Slobodian*

**Creatures Apart** | REVIEW 94
*Vivian Gornick*

**Plato and the Poets** | ESSAY 105
*Elaine Scarry*

**In Search of Arab Jews** | REVIEW 124
*Samuel Hayim Brody*

**The Real Path to Abundance** | REVIEW 144
*Sandeep Vaheesan*

CONTRIBUTORS 163

# EDITORS' NOTE

**THIS SECOND ISSUE OF** our fiftieth year features longtime contributors (including Robin D. G. Kelley, Vivian Gornick, and Elaine Scarry), newer voices in the magazine, and a celebration of classics from the archive. But more than simply a compilation of writing by authors we are privileged to work with, the issue reflects a conviction that has animated our work for decades: the daunting challenges we face must be met by collective thought and action.

As a starting point, Kelley revisits Noam Chomsky's landmark essay, "The Responsibility of Intellectuals." Published in 1967 as the Vietnam War was rapidly escalating, Chomsky's injunction—"to speak the truth and to expose lies"—remains a powerful call to conscience, Kelley argues. But in the Vietnam era, the intellectuals supporting the war all believed that they *were* acting responsibly. Moreover, the privileges that Chomsky associated with intellectual life are in increasingly short supply. A campaign of McCarthyist repression has overtaken universities. Lies circulate unchecked, no matter how forcefully exposed.

In these conditions, Kelley takes inspiration from the antifascist and anticolonial struggles of the 1930s and '40s—particularly from the Black radicals who refused and resisted complicity in their own age of fascism and genocide. Like them, he concludes, "we need to stand in solidarity and fight for others as if our lives depended on it." Historian David Waldstreicher, Palestinian human rights lawyer Jennifer Zacharia, and political philosopher Martin O'Neill expand on what this moment requires—not just of intellectuals, but of journalists and of us all.

Movements will be part of any effort. Brandon Terry interviews political scientist Cathy Cohen, who has been involved in some of the most consequential social movements of our time, about what we're up against and how activists can do better. On electoral politics and policy, David Austin Walsh explains what Zohran Mamdani's triumph in the New York City mayoral primary means for the future of the Democratic Party, and Sandeep Vaheesan assesses the "abundance" agenda and how best to build where need is greatest. Two review essays explore personal accounts of ruptured social connections: Samuel Hayim Brody on memoirs of the Arab Jewish world destroyed by colonialism, and Vivian Gornick on the reissue of Shulamith Firestone's *Airless Spaces*, a work about mental illness—but in the end about the essential loneliness of the human condition.

We're grateful to our readers for the ongoing support, and to Naomi Klein, Susan Faludi, Jay Caspian Kang, Rick Perlstein, Ryu Spaeth, Lea Ypi, and Nathan Robinson for writing about their favorite *Boston Review* essays—from Chomsky's 2011 "Responsibility of Intellectuals, Redux," to Gornick's appeal to "honor the existence of the one not like ourselves," to Scarry's 2002 "Citizenship in Emergency," which transforms the actions of passengers on 9/11's Flight 93 into an urgent call for democratic accountability. "Why," she asks, "are we sitting quietly in our seats?"

Scarry has a new essay in this issue as well, challenging the conventional wisdom that Plato wanted to rid the just city of poets. She tries to get the story right; if we don't, we risk "cutting off philosophers from poetry's expressive resources"—in other words, severing politics from imagination.

Her essay echoes the words of Colombian President Gustavo Petro in Joelle Abi-Rached's trenchant essay on Gaza and the hypocrisy of the liberal international order. In a speech in July before leaders from the Global South, convened to hold Israel accountable for war crimes, Petro stressed the need to keep alive "the possibility of another kind of humanity, one that can love and think collectively." We're working to do our part. **BR**

# THE RESPONSIBILITY OF INTELLECTUALS IN THE AGE OF FASCISM AND GENOCIDE

*Robin D. G. Kelley*

Fourteen years ago, Noam Chomsky published "The Responsibility of Intellectuals, Redux" in these pages. He used the occasion of the tenth anniversary of 9/11 to revisit his classic 1967 essay on the subject, although the immediate occasion for the piece was the assassination of Osama bin Laden by U.S. Navy Seals. As the Obama administration (and much of America) celebrated, Chomsky exposed the operation as a violation of U.S. and international law. The singular goal was to kill bin Laden, not capture him and bring him to trial. There was no pretense of habeas corpus since his body was summarily dumped into the sea.

Chomsky thus reiterates his original contention that it is the "responsibility of intellectuals" to tell the truth about war—in this instance, the war on terror and the crimes of U.S. imperialism in the Middle East, Latin America, Asia, and Africa. Referring to decades of debate on the phrase, he notes, "The phrase is ambiguous: does it refer to intellectuals' moral responsibility as decent human beings in a position to use their privilege and status to advance the causes of freedom, justice, mercy, peace, and other such sentimental concerns? Or does it refer to the role they are expected to play, serving, not derogating, leadership and established institutions?" His answer was clear: intellectuals must be guided by conscience and refuse to be beholden to state interests, either out of political loyalty or ideological commitment or both.



**Chomsky's injunction to "speak the truth and to expose lies" feels incomplete today. Whatever power truth-telling might have had against fascism has been radically diminished.**

The original essay, penned by a thirty-seven-year-old Chomsky, was adapted from a talk he gave at Harvard Hillel Society in 1966 and published in the student journal *Mosaic*. A revised and expanded version appeared as a special supplement in the February 23, 1967, edition of the *New York Review of Books*. The essay is a razor-sharp critique of intellectuals who, by assuming the roles of "experts" and technocrats for the state, abandon all moral, ethical, and historical judgment in order to advance ruling class interests and U.S. hegemony. Chomsky takes aim at the scholars and bureaucrats who had advised the Kennedy and Johnson administrations on Vietnam and Cuba and had no qualms about lying to the press and general public. These were the liberal intellectuals of Pax Americana who touted free-market capitalism as the universal measure of modern civilization. Communism, socialism, or any such alternatives were dismissed as dangerous "ideology," beyond the pale of common sense. Chomsky insisted that it was the responsibility, if not the duty, of intellectuals "to expose the lies of governments, to analyze actions according to their causes and motives and often hidden intentions."

Chomsky drew inspiration from a pair of essays by Dwight Macdonald in *politics* magazine in 1945. In a brief comment he would later retitle "The Responsibility of Intellectuals," Macdonald lampoons American journalist Max Lerner for wandering through postwar Germany asking ordinary people why they allowed Nazi atrocities to happen, all the while assuming an air of moral superiority and ignoring the role of the German state or the complicity of other Western powers. But Chomsky was primarily responding to "The Responsibility of Peoples," his longer, more nuanced essay, published a month earlier, critiquing the concept of collective war guilt. Macdonald observes that the conflation of "common peoples" with the interests and policies of nation-states corresponds with a devolution of their power and authority over their own government—what he termed "the dilemma of increasing political impotence accompanied by increasing political responsibility." This paradox not only fuels collective punishment but effectively relieves the "victors" of responsibility. As examples, Macdonald cites Allied carpet bombing, the nuclear destruction of Hiroshima and Nagasaki, and Japanese internment, as well as the crimes of colonial violence, lynching, and racial segregation. To blame all German people for Nazism, he concluded, is to blame all people for all atrocities, effectively occluding the specific operations of state violence and conflating compliance with universal consent, if not active support.

While Chomsky agreed with Macdonald's critique of collective guilt, he argued that intellectuals in Western democracies bear some moral responsibility by virtue of their privileged position. "In the Western world, at least," he contended, "they have the power that comes from political liberty, from access to information and freedom of expression." This privilege affords intellectuals unique opportunities to speak out. "Opportunity," he adds in his 2011 redux, "confers responsibilities. An individual then has choices."

Of course, Chomsky knew that such "privilege" was hardly universal—that dissenting without fear of state violence eluded dissident intellectuals in other parts of the world. Graveyards and gulags are filled with intellectuals who tried to exercise their "moral responsibility" to tell the truth. Even in the "liberal" United States, prison or exile has been the fate of generations of radical thinkers, especially those from marginalized communities. Who can speak, when, on what subjects, and from what platforms is determined by historical context and differentiated by race, gender, class, ideology, and politics. Individuals may have choices, but they are constrained by social and political conditions. In times of crisis, war, and fascism, opportunities open or close depending on where one stands in relation to the ruling power. We do not now—and never did—live in a world, or a nation, dominated by independent iconoclasts, tenured radicals, or dedicated philosophes pursuing knowledge free from politics.





On the contrary, dissidents or insurgents represent just a tiny fraction of what is erroneously called "the intellectual class." Chomsky believed that the intellectuals who fully backed the ruling regime had somehow betrayed their duty or obligation to expose the administration's lies. I think it is more accurate to say that they thought they were fulfilling their duty, but their choices were ideologically and politically driven. As they saw it, their responsibility was to defend U.S. foreign policy *because they believed it was right*: there was no need to expose facts or disclose the truth because the threat of communism is what mattered. The problem, that is, was not an absence of moral courage but a dedication to Cold War liberalism.

By the time Chomsky revisited his essay in 2011, he had not only become a much sharper critic of liberalism. Neoliberalism had also reshaped higher education. The university's embrace of market fundamentalism is now totally complete, and the creeping privatization of public universities has seen corporate donors, higher tuitions, and questionable investments replace shrinking state funding. Top administrators are no longer beholden to students and faculty, the pursuit of knowledge, or the public good but to donors, trustees, and government. For the last couple of decades, we've seen a growing assault on critical inquiry, academic freedom, and safety, alongside the casualization of labor, rising tuitions, severe budget cuts to humanities and other non-STEM fields, and the financialization of higher education. Finance capital has become a silent driver of university policy, and conservative state legislatures have imposed additional limits and mandates on higher education in their respective states. As a consequence, the "privilege" that Chomsky recognized in 1967 now eludes many insurgent academics. And another privilege he recognized—access to information—has been dispersed with the internet.

The political context is different, too. At a time when lies, deceptions, and fake news are so entrenched that critics have dubbed ours the "post-truth era," we are facing a global turn toward authoritarianism, rising fascism in the United States, mounting political violence, multiple genocides, and a relentless right-wing attack on critical knowledge, colleges and universities, and basic liberal education. With the help of the United States, Israel continues to massacre, starve, and displace Gaza's civilian population under the pretense of self-defense. We are witnessing genocide. We are living in fascist times.





Under these conditions, the possibilities that Chomsky saw in the power of truth-telling from privileged intellectuals are vastly diminished. But more than that, our situation helps us to see that there was always something misformulated about Chomsky's question, however forcefully it exposed the moral bankruptcy of the "value-free" experts who perpetrated war in Vietnam. Those intellectuals aligned with the state were always going to lie, since they had chosen their side. The real questions before us are: What is the responsibility of intellectuals *committed* to fighting fascism and genocide? How do we refuse and resist complicity when our own institutions are complicit? And what might we learn from earlier antifascist and anticolonial struggles?

---

**TO BEGIN TO ANSWER** these questions, it is instructive to return to the notion of the "organic intellectual" developed by the Italian Marxist Antonio Gramsci in his *Prison Notebooks*, written between 1929 and 1935 while he was imprisoned by the Mussolini regime. "It is difficult to find a single criterion to characterize equally well all the disparate activities of intellectuals and, at the same time, distinguish them and in an essential way from the activities of other social groups," Gramsci wrote:

> The most widespread methodological error, it seems to me, has been to look for the essential characteristic in the intrinsic nature of intellectual activity rather than in the system of relations wherein this activity (and group that personifies it) is located in the general ensemble of social relations.

By "ensemble," Gramsci wasn't just referring to class relations but to the whole range of identities and institutions that shape our place in society. Because every human being has the capacity to think critically and possesses a worldview formed from experience, Gramsci insisted that all people are intellectuals, but they do not all function as such in society. "Traditional" intellectuals—for Gramsci, the teachers, scholars, clergy, and other figures who imagined themselves occupying an autonomous position in the social world—play a critical role in maintaining the hegemony of the dominant class, shaping ideology, law, culture, and "common sense," organizing consent, and stifling class antagonisms. "Organic" intellectuals, by contrast, are embedded in specific classes or social groups, reflecting as well as articulating the interests and ideology of their class. To them, the responsibility of intellectuals is to choose a side and fight.



We tend to associate organic intellectuals with what Gramsci refers to as "subaltern" groups—the oppressed, marginalized, and exploited classes. But the dominant classes also have their organic intellectuals, as do right-wing and fascist movements contesting for power—all of whom also see it as their responsibility to analyze and critique the social order from the standpoint of their class or social group, educate, build and hold power, lay out a vision of a future rooted in their movement's collective imagination, and fight to bring it into existence. In other words, they are not just cogs in a machine beyond their control but ideologues who create, drive, and justify policy in the interests of their class or political bloc.

In 1967, Chomsky was writing as a kind of organic intellectual with many of the privileges typically reserved for traditional intellectuals. As a tenured professor at MIT, the epicenter of the nation's burgeoning academic-military complex, he managed to say and write what he wanted—including severe criticism of the liberal ruling class around him and in Washington—without professional or legal consequences. (Not that he didn't experience blowback: he was always widely reviled by the mainstream media and was arrested for an antiwar teach-in outside the Pentagon in 1967, for example.)

At the time, the American professoriate was overwhelmingly white and male. Cold War expansion turned leading universities into the research and development arm of corporations and the warfare state, thanks in large part to federal grants and foundations. But as more universities began opening their doors to women and students of color, the struggles in the streets and the world spilled over onto campuses. Universities were hardly engines of change, but they increasingly became contested terrain. Chomsky's initial talk reflected growing student discontent with U.S. foreign policy and its publication paralleled the rise of an explosive student movement: resisting the draft, demanding new forms of democracy, opening the vaunted doors of academia to the people, breaking universities' ties with imperialism, and launching new forms of inquiry—Black Studies, Ethnic Studies, Women's Studies.

And yet, a wider problem looms over his *New York Review* essay like a faint shadow: fascism. It was Macdonald's musings on fascism and war that drew Chomsky to the question of responsibility in the first place—subjects Macdonald would ponder for years to come. Indeed, when "The Responsibility of Peoples" appeared in his 1953 book, *The Root Is Man: Two Essays in Politics*, Macdonald added the following footnote:

> By an ironical twist of history, the victims have now become oppressors in their turn. Since 1948, some 800,000 Arab refugees, who fled from Palestine during the fighting, have been living wretchedly in camps around the country's borders maintained by UN charity. The Israeli government—opposed by no important Jewish group that I know of—refuses to let them back and has given their homes, farms, and villages to new Jewish settlers. This is rationalized by the usual 'collective responsibility' nonsense. This expropriation cannot, of course, be put on the same plane as the infinitely greater crime of the Nazis. But neither should it be passed over in silence.

Today this passage would be considered antisemitic, its author subject to investigation, libelous condemnation by the Anti-Defamation League (ADL), and possible dismissal. But so long as Macdonald forswore communism, he was free to exercise his "privilege" as an intellectual.

Chomsky makes no mention of this footnote in his *New York Review* essay, but he heeds Macdonald's message that wars of dispossession and ethnic cleansing should never "be passed over in silence." And he, too, turns to the analogy of Nazi Germany to make sense of Vietnam, likening U.S. aggression "with a fanatic belief in its manifest destiny" to Hitler.

"Of course, the aggressiveness of liberal imperialism is not that of Nazi Germany," Chomsky writes, "though the distinction may seem academic to a Vietnamese peasant who is being gassed or incinerated."

**We are witnessing levels of repression not seen since the Red Scare.**





Still, the imminent threat of fascism back home goes notably unaddressed. Treating intellectuals as an autonomous social category, Chomsky sidesteps their differential relationship to, and embeddedness within, social relations. Three weeks after "The Responsibility of Intellectuals" appeared, Dr. Martin Luther King, Jr., published an account of the Chicago Freedom Movement's 1966 march for open housing in which he compared the mob violence they encountered to that of Nazi Germany. "Swastikas bloomed in Chicago parks like misbegotten weeds," he wrote. "Our marchers were met by a hailstorm of bricks, bottles, and firecrackers. 'White power' became the racist hatecall, punctuated by obscenities." Later that summer, police violence sparked massive rebellions in Detroit, Newark, and over 150 cities, prompting state officials to send National Guard troops to occupy Black neighborhoods. The Black Panther Party declared U.S. state violence "fascist" and in 1969 organized a United Front Against Fascism conference in Oakland, California, in addition to forming the National Committee to Combat Fascism to resist police repression.

Black and brown struggles against homegrown fascism were not Chomsky's focus at the time. This is perfectly understandable: he was concerned mainly with the crimes of American empire and colonial violence abroad. In fact, years later Chomsky explained that part of the reason for the focus of his Harvard talk was that McGeorge Bundy, who had served as dean there, had been an enthusiastic supporter of the Vietnam war as President Johnson's national security advisor. But as a long line of Black radicals had argued, colonial violence abroad was closely linked with fascism at home. To understand this relationship, we need to pay attention to the longer history of antifascism, particularly the role of Black organic intellectuals in the 1930s and '40s—when politics, media, and intellectual production more closely resembled the highly partisan landscape of our own time than the postwar liberal ideal of objectivity and consensus that prevailed when Chomsky was writing.

---

**In that period,** antifascism not only drew students and faculty out of the universities and into the streets, union halls, unemployed councils, communist and socialist parties, and the battlefields of Spain. It also brought antifascism and varieties of Marxism—Trotskyism, Stalinism, Fabian Socialism—into the university. The largely Jewish working-class campus of City College in New York became a hotbed of socialist and antifascist organizing. Even pristine Columbia University became a major site of antifascist protest when its president, Nicholas Murray Butler, welcomed Nazi Germany's ambassador to the United States to speak on campus in December 1933. The more than 1,000 students and allies who showed up to disrupt the speech confronted police wielding billy clubs. But they were not deterred. Students called on the administration to publicly rebuke the Nazi regime, boycott German goods, assist German refugees, and hire exiled scholars. Butler, a longtime admirer of Mussolini who had established ties between Columbia and Italy, remained steadfast for several years, electing to crush student dissent rather than disavow fascism.

Left-wing, anticolonial, antifascist, and civil rights organizations had their share of Black organic intellectuals whose activism and writing reshaped scholarship and politics in the U.S. The writings of W. E. B. Du Bois, C. L. R. James, Louise Thompson Patterson, George Padmore, Claudia Jones, Marvel Cooke, Ella Baker, Abram Harris, Richard Wright, young Ralph Bunche, and many others, were not produced in isolation but in relation to movement and as conscious efforts to combat fascism, racism, and colonialism. Indeed, they recognized that fascism was *born of* racism and colonialism. Their mobilizations against the Italian invasion of Ethiopia in 1935, as American business leaders and university presidents such as Butler feted Mussolini, were among the first antifascist actions in the United States. They called out and resisted homegrown fascism in the form of lynch law, the suppression of workers' organizations and virtually all forms of dissent, and the denial of civil and democratic rights to Black citizens. As poet, playwright, essayist, and activist Langston Hughes told those assembled at the Third U.S. Congress against War and Fascism in 1936, "Fascism is a new name for that kind of terror the Negro has always faced in America. . . . This kind of terrorism is extending more and more to groups of peoples whose skins are not black."



The early life and work of sociologist St. Clair Drake is exemplary of this generation of organic intellectuals whose work shaped, and was shaped by, opposition to fascism and colonialism. Son of a Garveyite father from Barbados and a mother from Virginia, Drake came to activism through the pacificism of the Quakers. Four years after graduating from Hampton Institute in 1931, he went to Dillard University in New Orleans to work as a research assistant and teach, all the while immersing himself in antifascist and pacifist politics. He worked with the NAACP and published articles in *The Crisis*, the organization's official magazine, on lynching and the antiwar movement. In May 1936, he and two other Black Dillard faculty members, Lawrence Reddick and Byron Augustine, joined local NAACP Secretary James LaFourche to disrupt a massive pro-fascist parade organized by the city's Italian community. The men boldly drove a car through the line of march bearing a placard that read "We Protest Against the Celebration of Aggressive War and Fascism." Police surrounded the car and allowed the marchers to tear up the sign but no one was arrested. Drake left the following year to pursue graduate work at the University of Chicago, continuing to organize against fascism, before returning to Dillard in 1941. He didn't last long; within a year he was fired for supporting student protests against bus segregation.

Drake went on to coauthor, with fellow sociologist Horace R. Cayton, Jr., *Black Metropolis*, a landmark two-volume study of Chicago's South Side, also known as Bronzeville. While the book broke new ground in the study of Black life, what I find particularly striking is its consistent antifascist politics: there is no pretense of detachment or effort to conceal its political stakes. Published in 1946, when Black men who had helped defeat fascism faced unemployment and an uptick in racist violence, the authors predicted that "the Negro may again become a chronic relief client, despised by the majority of white citizens who have to support him from taxes and the symbol around which the aggressions of a frustrated society can be organized, so that he may fill the role of the whipping boy for an emerging American Fascism." Such an outcome could be avoided, they argued, so long as the United States achieved full employment and the entire world embraced, in their words, a "program for emancipating the Common Man." "The problems that arise on Bronzeville's Forty-seventh Street encircle the globe," they wrote. "A blow struck for freedom in Bronzeville finds its echo in Chungking and Moscow, in Paris and Senegal. A victory for Fascism in Midwest Metropolis will sound the knell of doom for the Common Man everywhere."





Drake and Cayton understood that defeating Germany and Japan would not end fascism at home. In an opinion piece for the *Pittsburgh Courier* dated May 19, 1945, Cayton wrote, "We now turn to the war within our own country. Victory for democracy will mean some chance of a peace. Victory for our own native Fascism—the Hitler which lives in us—will mean that we're setting the stage for the next world war." His warning was echoed by Black Communist Party leader Claudia Jones, who argued in a 1946 article that fascism was alive and well in the Jim Crow South, evidenced in part by the revival of lynching and the beatings and assassinations of Black veterans. "Today the main danger of fascism to the world comes from the most colossal imperialist forces which are concentrated within the United States," Jones observed. "The perpetrators of these attacks are the representatives of the most reactionary section of monopoly capital and of the semi-feudal economy of the Black Belt."

The West claimed victory over fascism even as it continued to perpetuate fascist and genocidal policies in the colonies, semi-colonies, and ghettoes. In 1945, three years before the Afrikaner-led National Party came to power and implemented apartheid, the Non-European Unity Movement, a multiracial Trotskyist-led organization opposed to white minority rule, issued a powerful statement comparing life in South Africa to the Third Reich: "The Non Europeans of South Africa live and suffer under a tyranny very little different from Nazism. And if we accept that there can be no peace as long as the scourge of Nazism exists in any corner of the globe, then it follows that the defeat of German Nazism is not the final chapter of the struggle against tyranny." Aimé Césaire's *Discourse on Colonialism*, first published in 1950, not only joined other radical thinkers in identifying the seeds of fascism in the colonial order but pointed to the atrocities committed by French occupation forces in response to anticolonial resistance as evidence of fascism's persistence. "Think of it!" Césaire intoned. "Ninety thousand dead in Madagascar! Indochina trampled underfoot, crushed to bits, assassinated, tortures brought back from the depths of the Middle Ages!"

**A long line of Black radicals argued that violence abroad was closely linked with fascism at home.**



In 1951, William L. Patterson, executive director of the Civil Rights Congress (CRC) and a leading member of the Communist Party, attempted to submit a copy of *We Charge Genocide!: The Crime of Government Against the Negro People*, a book-length study of American state-sanctioned racial violence, to a UN delegation in Paris. Paul Robeson simultaneously attempted to submit the same text to the UN in New York. Drafted by Patterson, Richard Boyer, Elizabeth Lawson, Yvonne Gregory, Oakley Johnson, and Aubrey Grossman, *We Charge Genocide!* not only documented hundreds of incidents of anti-Black violence during the six years since the end of World War II; it also served as a petition to the UN indicting the United States for violating both the UN Charter and its 1948 Convention on Genocide. Patterson did not believe that the UN could ensure world peace so long as modern democracies promoted racism at home and colonialism abroad. If the United States, the most powerful nation on the planet after World War II, could continue to subject African Americans to what amounted to a fascist order, then world peace was illusory. The UN could easily become a smokescreen for American imperialism. "We cannot forget Hitler's demonstration," reads the opening statement, "that genocide at home can become wider massacre abroad, that domestic genocide develops into the larger genocide that is predatory war. The wrongs of which we complain are so much the expression of predatory American reaction and its government that civilization cannot ignore them nor risk their continuance without courting its own destruction."

The UN never seriously considered the document. Eleanor Roosevelt, then the U.S. representative to the UN Human Rights Commission, as well as Black delegates Edith Sampson and Channing Tobias, condemned *We Charge Genocide!*. The U.S. State Department viewed Patterson's actions as libelous and possibly criminal. When Patterson refused an order from the U.S. Embassy to surrender his passport, he fled France and was ultimately detained in Britain. His passport was revoked as soon as he returned to the United States, sharing the same fate as his friends Paul Robeson and W. E. B. Du Bois. A little over two years later, Patterson would also be jailed for refusing to turn over the CRC's receipt books.





The story of Black antifascism and resistance to genocide doesn't end here, but it is worth pausing to consider the fates of Patterson, Du Bois, and Robeson for exercising what they believed was their responsibility to expose and resist fascism. We might include C. L. R. James and Claudia Jones, both of whom were deported for their political work. Black insurgent intellectuals warned the nation and the world, took principled stances against fascism when it wasn't popular, spoke truth to power from a position of marginality, and fought for an oppressed class—a large proportion of which would not fight for them.

---

**TO RETURN, THEN,** to the urgent question: What is the responsibility of intellectuals in the age of fascism and genocide? Certainly, Chomsky's ending to his 1967 essay continues to ring true: an individual with privilege has choices. But one must choose sides, and as we have seen, opportunities for acting depend on where one stands in relation to the ruling power. On campuses over the past few decades, dissident intellectuals have increasingly faced growing hostility and silencing. And now, in our fascist moment, we are witnessing levels of repression not seen since the Red Scare.

For decades the new economic precarity for academics has worked in conjunction in particular with repression of criticism of Israel to silence truth-telling. At least since the launch of the Boycott, Divestment, Sanctions Movement (BDS) in 2004, American colleges and universities have been relentless in their suppression of Palestine advocacy. For his criticism of Israel, Norman Finkelstein was denied tenure at DePaul University in 2007. Those of us who have been fighting for Palestine's freedom are familiar with the Canary Mission website posting names of people it falsely accuses of antisemitism, or the practice of doxxing, or the ADL's long history of spying on progressive organizations. The David Horowitz Freedom Center (DHFC) spent years plastering campuses with posters accusing students and faculty *by name* of terrorism and "Jew hatred." Since it started operating in 2002 the Israel on Campus Coalition (ICC) has boasted its direct ties to Israeli intelligence and to AIPAC, collected information on Palestine solidarity organizations, assembled dossiers on targeted students and faculty, and passed them on to Israel's Ministry of Strategic Affairs. Data collected from the ICC is then fed to the ADL, which it uses to monitor and attack critics of Israel and produce an annual report: "Anti-Israel Activism on U.S. Campuses."



The intensity and scope of the repression escalated after October 7 as university administrators started firing and suspending faculty, rescinding job offers, surveilling classrooms, expanding campus security forces, and calling police to clear Palestine solidarity encampments and arrest students. Since then hundreds of academics who have stood with student protesters, voiced criticism of Israel, or insisted that Palestinian lives be given equal value have been disciplined, assaulted, arrested, sued, harassed, doxxed, and dismissed. Thanks to the work of Palestine Legal, Academics for Palestine, and Faculty for Justice in Palestine, we know their names: Anne D'Aquino, Mohamed Abdou, Eman Abdelhadi, Ruha Benjamin, Graeme Blair, Jodi Dean, Caroline Fohlin, Amin Husain, Sang Hea Kil, Noëlle McAfee, Annelise Orleck, Steven Thrasher, Danny Shaw, and Tiffany Willoughby-Herard, to name just a few. Most of those who were dismissed were untenured, although tenure did not protect Maura Finklestein, Rupa Marya, and Katherine Franke from being fired or forced into early retirement.

By suppressing criticisms of Israel and campus protests and capitulating to donor demands, university administrators violated the principles of academic freedom and therefore undermined their moral authority and political standing. University administrators, most having risen from the ranks of the faculty, are also intellectuals; as such, they too have a moral responsibility and "choices." But like state intellectuals, they believe they are beholden to the interests of the university. Confronted with trustees and donors who not only threaten to withhold funds but demand severe punishments for student protesters and conspire with the corporate and legal world to deny them future employment, administrators chose to cower before such pressure rather than stand up for the rights, well-being, and safety of their own students. Capitulating to donors paved the way for capitulating to Trump.

Accusations of antisemitism thus became the pretext for the Trump administration to withhold hundreds of millions of dollars of federal grants from colleges and universities. Of course, given the influence of white Christian nationalists and white supremacists among the MAGA base, the image of Trump protecting the Jewish community strains credulity. For Christian Zionists and right-wing evangelicals, antisemitism is tolerable, and the final solution is prophesy: Christ will appear in the Second Coming and destroy nearly all of mankind, including the vast majority of Jews. The born again will be "raptured" into the clouds out of danger, and, when the battle is over, will rejoin Jesus and inherit the Holy Land. Jews who survive will then have to accept Christ as their lord and savior. Antisemitic Zionism may not be new, but the use of the U.S. state to advance the Zionist project is unprecedented.

The Heritage Foundation provided the model for the administration's aggressive attacks on Israel's critics with Project Esther, a "national strategy to combat antisemitism" that in turn takes its entire playbook from the Cold War "experts" who deceived America about Vietnam: if you can't win the argument, lie. Drafted in the wake of the October 7 attacks, the plan intends to crush what it deems "anti-Israel" protests by labeling all critics of Israel and Zionism antisemites, Marxists, and terrorists with direct ties to Hamas. The authors use every possible platform—social media, online publications, letter-writing, websites—to accuse groups such as Jewish Voice for Peace, National Students for Justice in Palestine, and Alliance for Global Justice of being a "Hamas Support Organization" (HSO) or part of a "Hamas Support Network" (HSN). In other words, the strategy is to knowingly lie and see what sticks. The document lays out a detailed plan to delegitimize and criminalize critics of Israel through lawfare, dig up evidence of "criminal wrongdoing" through financial audits and public records requests, spread propaganda "designed to illuminate and expose—'name and shame,'—to undermine HSN and HSO members' credibility," and pressure federal authorities to revoke the visas of and deport international students who criticize Israel or its war on Gaza.

Even Harvard University, held up as the only major institution of higher education to stand up to the Trump administration after it canceled some $3.2 billion dollars in grants and contracts, has now quietly taken steps to conform with the new political reality. It replaced its office for diversity, equity, and inclusion and with "Community and Campus Life"; suspended a research partnership between Harvard's School of Public Health and Birzeit University in the West Bank; removed two prominent scholars, Cemal Kafadar and Rosie Bsheer, director and associate director respectively, from running the Center for Middle Eastern Studies (CMES); and pushed out the leadership of the Divinity School's Religion and Public Life Program and its affiliate, the Religion, Conflict, and Peace Initiative (RCPI). By spring 2025, the university had suspended RCPI, firing Atalia Omer, a Jewish Israeli scholar of religion who works on Israel/Palestine peacebuilding, and Hilary Rantisi, the program's associate director and the only Palestinian staff member in the Divinity School.

Of course, the repression of U.S. scholars does not compare to what Palestinian scholars in Palestine have had to endure. Oxford University Professor Karma Nabulsi coined the term "scholasticide" to describe Israel's ongoing war on intellectuals, intellectual life, and academic institutions in Gaza, the West Bank, and East Jerusalem. Since the start of the war, every college and university in Gaza has been destroyed, and thousands of professors, administrators, schoolteachers, and students have been killed, wounded, or jailed.

Meanwhile, MAGA has been forging a robust community of its own organic intellectuals and benefitting from their work. Philosopher Jason Stanley correctly observes that universities are among the first targets of fascist attacks. However, when we pit "intellectuals" or the university against the Trump regime, as if "reason" or the lack thereof is the primary antagonism, we commit a grave error. Stephen Miller, Steve Bannon, Christopher Rufo, Peter Brimelow, Curtis Yarvin, Michael Anton, Jason Richwine, and the army of scholars and policy wonks behind the Heritage Foundation's Project 2025 all play a significant role in MAGA's success. Many of these figures are leading proponents of eugenics and other manifestations of discredited race science, which provide the intellectual scaffolding for mass deportations targeting Latinx, Caribbean, African, and Asian immigrants, while extending refugee status to white South Africans. Anton, who served as senior national security official during Trump's first term and was appointed Director of Policy Planning at the State Department in his second term, made the case for ending birthright citizenship, arguing in part that diversity is "a source of weakness, tension and disunion. America is not a 'nation of immigrants'; we are originally a nation of settlers, who later chose to admit immigrants."

**Defeating fascism requires recognizing that we need to stand in solidarity and fight for others as if our lives depended on it.**



To be clear, the Biden administration had much in common with the first Trump administration from a policy standpoint, particularly with respect to immigration and its promotion of war across the planet, from its anti-China saber rattling to its support for (or indifference to) genocidal violence in Sudan, Eastern Congo, Haiti, and Palestine. Nevertheless, MAGA's organic intellectuals have helped create a new fascist political bloc representing the interests of billionaires, fossil fuel corporations, cryptocurrency magnates, Silicon Valley, Christian nationalists, and white supremacists. Their broad agenda entails eliminating the social safety net, trade unions, affordable health care, public health safeguards, trans people, civil and disability rights, academic freedom, and investment in renewable energy, promoting the mass deportation of immigrants, deregulating anything that might hinder capital accumulation (including fossil fuel extraction and generative AI), reorganizing and privatizing education—all with the quite explicit goal of remaking the United States in the image of whiteness.

In these conditions, Chomsky's injunction to choose dissent, to "speak the truth and to expose lies," feels incomplete. To be sure, Chomsky harbored no illusions about the need to build a movement powerful enough to take on the ruling class, but the public memory of his essay has ossified into misleading mantra. Whatever power truth-telling might have had against fascism has been radically diminished. There is ample scholarship proving that immigrants do not take jobs, that they are not responsible for low wages, that war in Gaza doesn't make Jews safe, that the 2020 election wasn't stolen, that the United States is not a benevolent agent of democracy promotion, that antiracism is not hating America. The right can pull out its own "evidence," make up authoritative stories, use emotions rather than cold reason; they are not bound by so-called liberal values and have said so. Besides, liberals themselves bear some responsibility for this catastrophe. As former State Department spokesman Matthew Miller recently admitted, "I think it is, without a doubt, true that Israel has committed war crimes." Miller had tenaciously defended Israel's onslaught in Gaza before the press corps. But as he explained, "When you're at the podium, you're not expressing your personal opinion. You're expressing the conclusions of the United States government."

What we can do is what generations of antifascist intellectuals, from Gramsci to Cayton to Claudia Jones, did eighty years ago and after: cast our lot with the insurgent class and enter the struggle. In the words of Maurice Mitchell, national director of the Working Families Party, "It's not enough to have just done the reading or even tell compelling stories. . . . We need to put it into practice in and with our communities." There are so many movements to plug into, from fighting for tenants' rights, affordable housing, disability and reproductive justice, and trans rights; resisting ICE raids; joining the Debt Collective or the Poor People's Campaign in their fight for a livable future; supporting independent left think tanks such as the Hampton Institute, the People's Policy Project, the Institute for Policy Studies, or the Tricontinental Institute for Social Research; to building political capacity through groups like the Working Families Party.

Moving beyond the ivory tower does not mean abandoning the university. The university is still contested terrain, and groups such as Scholars for Social Justice, the African American Policy Forum, and the Smart Cities Lab have managed to carve out spaces for resistance and visionary planning from within. UCLA's Institute on Inequality and Democracy, founded by Ananya Roy, is an exemplary model of what insurgent intellectual work can look like. For the last ten years, the Institute has not only effectively fought for affordable housing and against racial banishment but developed a dynamic activist-in-residence program to provide space for movement intellectuals—from South Africa to Chicago to here in Los Angeles—to think with scholars in order to better understand the forces pushing people into greater precarity and find ways to fight back.

In order to sustain this work, we need to create a new university. And we will never change anything unless we are organized. Unionizing all faculty and teaching staff is not just about salaries and teaching loads, but about academic freedom, free speech, and the right to protest. Our efforts to build solidarity on campuses have tended to be around something bigger, about values and intervening in the world. Yes, we do this in our classrooms all the time, which is why the state and our university admins try to monitor everything we do. But it's when we seek to build power, expand governance, take the offensive, and recognize our responsibility to transform this world, that the hammer falls. And the myth of the liberal university, of the transcendent intellectual, of the power of reason shatters at once. The lesson is that defeating the fascism we face now requires much more than defeating the current administration or winning elections. It requires a deeper shift: the recognition that we need to always stand in solidarity and fight for others as if our lives depended on it.

On May 16 last year, Howard Gilman, Chancellor of the University of California, Irvine, called the police to disperse what had been a peaceful Palestine solidarity encampment. My friend and colleague, Global Studies Professor Tiffany Willoughby-Herard, was standing with her students in an effort to protect them when three cops pushed her down on the concrete and cuffed her. Escorted by two officers, she was caught on video as local media attempted to interview her. "We cannot have a genocidal foreign policy in a democracy," she cried:

> These young people are going to be the ones that have to pay the price for these horrible decisions. These police officers out here today, that's thousands of students' scholarships. Thousands of students that could have been able to go to school and have books and have housing. But instead, our Chancellor, who is a very cruel man, decided to send thousands of dollars' worth of state funding paid for by the taxpayers into the trash.

When asked if she was concerned about jeopardizing her job, she replied in a single sentence that still brings tears to my eyes: "What job do I have if the students don't have a future?"

In sixty seconds, while being zip-tied and dragged away by riot police, Willoughby-Heard put in bold relief the question at the heart of this essay: What is our responsibility in the face of fascism and genocide? Her very presence in struggle, putting her body and her future on the line, answered the question. **BR**

# On the Responsibility of Historians

## *David Waldstreicher*

**INTELLECTUALS ALWAYS** have responsibilities, and historians are surely part of what most people mean when they speak of that class. What is our role at the present time?

I begin with a confession: I've never been comfortable with the mantle of intellectual. It joins one to some but mostly sets one apart. Besides, for more than two decades I have taught at public universities. My classroom is for everyone; my expertise is a public good, paid for, in admittedly ever-decreasing part, by taxpayer dollars. As a caretaker of knowledge, in my case about our common national history, I'm in the truth business, but funded by and for the collective. Dwelling on my difference—a special sense of responsibility that accrues to my role as an intellectual, modified by other identities and loyalties—strikes me as self-indulgent.

Yet in a regime that targets intellectuals as fellow travelers with all the wrong people, one no longer needs to theorize the student, the teacher, the academic, the writer, as a marginalized person or exile-at-home, as sociologists and movement makers were doing when Noam Chomsky wrote his classic essay in 1967. In retrospect, perhaps the most striking thing about his conception of his subject is his certainty about who he is talking about. Permit me, then, to trace some history.

There was a discourse then about The Intellectual, that airy figure conceived as heir both to the Enlightenment and to modernism, as well as a parallel, more specific discourse about the responsibility of the Black intellectual to his—as the assumption at the time invariably went—"community." The postwar U.S. state was caught in the contradiction of having expanded the university to accommodate the GIs, the baby boomers, and the Cold War only to find that it had wound up funding and creating spaces for opposition along the way. The campus, as a demographically skewed little city, became a site of real political agitation and controversy and hand-wringing as well as generational conflict. It also began training a larger, more diverse class of intellectuals with higher degrees—a class that, as it mushroomed, came to seem more secure and bourgeois (as opposed to shabby-aristocratic) than an earlier professoriate and not necessarily all that intellectual, if by that we mean, as Chomsky did, critical and interested in politics and culture beyond one's academic specialty. For several decades, Chomsky's choice between speaking truth to power and justifying the status quo came to seem less stark or necessary than it did in 1967. Most writers and professors existed comfortably in an expanding middle or grey zone where tough choices, or agitations, seemed either unnecessary or someone else's job.

Ever since, intellectuals have drawn agonized circles around the results. The transformation seemed, and felt, both natural and weird. Surely academe wasn't the real world, its denizens, whether temporary or tenured, not "the people." Yet that world continued to grow, continued to matter and to attract money too, even as it mocked itself in a subgenre of campus novels and suffered the arrival of "late capitalism" in the form of funding crises at state universities. The right grumbled about "tenured radicals"; radicals muttered "As if!" or replied with ironic manifestos. The rise of the so-called "knowledge economy" in the 1990s muddied distinctions further. As president, Barack Obama made higher education sound like a middle-class right while trying to turn the narrative toward workforce development, away from his own origins as a Columbia student turned community organizer turned law professor turned legislator.

By then, higher ed looked polarized as a public policy matter, the Democratic Party identified with both its public and private forms and the GOP increasingly arrayed against it. The academy too felt increasingly politicized, intellectual life itself more performative, riskier, and certainly more alienated than in its heady years of expansion, especially in light of the at first creeping, then overwhelming adjunctification of the faculty. Canon and "culture" wars flared, punctuated by the small wars that seemed designed to elect presidents and frustrate comparisons to Vietnam and the 1960s. Some might have remembered their wartime predecessors, like Charles Beard in 1917 and W. E. B. Du Bois in 1944 and Staughton Lynd in 1969, who had been effectively forced out of the academy for their politics even while their intellectual work anticipated emerging trends.

All that seems a pale shadow, a mere foreshadow, of what we face now. Today the Trump administration is putting its heavy thumb over the academy and everything it is supposed to be good for: making citizens, doing research, exploring new ideas. In the name of restoring a mythically glorious (read: white) past, congressional inquisitors are undermining the very autonomy of the life of the mind from the meddling influence of the state, the freedoms of teaching and research, that have always represented the best of what the American university has had to offer. The very fact that people all over the world wish to come here to further their education (and even help pay the bills) makes the university epitomize for the nativist right everything that has gone wrong with the country and its thinking classes. The professor is now not merely a potential homegrown dissident: they are figured in this reactionary fantasy as an urban migrant displacing the heartland stock from its rightful place in the cultural elite and poisoning the homeland with their "DEI" or "terrorist" words. The siege has all the contradictions of every Herrenvolk campaign. Invoking scarcity of the right's own creation—competition for limited funds and limited spaces—the imagined solution, as usual, is not to expand and include, still less to make a brief for anything free, universal, and public, but to oust and expel and extort.

There are precedents within U.S. history, during wartime and at the state level. Whether we call it fascism or note the parallels with contemporary Hungary, India, or Hong Kong, suppression is both first move and endgame, whether operating through funding freezes, police actions on campus, or a Department of Justice that has flipped the meaning of discrimination on its head.

In this situation I see it as the particular responsibility of the intellectual in the United States to testify from experience, as well as knowledge, that this moment of rank repression and corruption is at once recurrent—continuous with a pattern running through U.S. history—and unprecedented in scope and form as the immediate result of a presidential election. The Democrats, as a party, still refuse to admit the glaring violence behind their loss: another Middle East war, which Bidenites enabled. This was Gulf War and 9/11 redux—the third time as genocide. As the late Amy Kaplan made so clear in *Our American Israel* (2018), the current conjuncture of domestic politics and international alliances reflects a heightening of trends going back more than half a century, issuing from generations of fantasy about American and Israeli innocence. Among its perverse effects has been to provide cover for a presidential administration populated by officials with links to antisemitic white nationalism to carry out a siege on the academy under the rubric of anti-antisemitism, all while drawing support from the likes of the Anti-Defamation League.

Nothing confirms Chomsky's distinction between responsible intellectuals and functionaries of the state like the current trend of college administrators rushing to strike deals with the federal government to placate The Leader. The headline on the July 14 cover story of the *Philadelphia Inquirer* put it directly: "The art of the deal between Penn and Trump." The kowtowing, at Penn and Brown and Columbia and beyond, will be familiar to anyone who watches university administrators; DEI programs have been toppling everywhere under much less pressure. But it is unconscionably short-term thinking and action, taken with apparently no historical or political awareness of what happens, in business or politics or everyday life, when one agrees to what is in essence bullying and extortion, or accepts rules of war that can be changed at any time. What will they demand, and take, tomorrow? And who next will pay the price?

The immediate material stakes are high, but this battle is also as symbolic as they come. The dispatching of fighting forces on the streets and the relishing in sheer violence go hand in hand with the assault on intellectual life, which is hardly an afterthought or mere collateral damage. Rather, it is a culmination of what Richard Slotkin names "The Age of Culture War." In privileging their budgets and abandoning guardrails around free speech, the richest institutions in the country demonstrate that they are not interested in the responsibility of intellectuals felt keenly by their own systematically disempowered, if privileged, faculty. They fail to ask why the regime, spurred by its would-be inheritors like J. D. Vance and Stephen Miller and Christopher Rufo, is making such a priority of cracking down on higher education as well as immigrants, and what that already has meant for those downstream of the repression of both protest on campus and academic self-governance, especially in states with compliant red legislatures.

In other words, the university is now center stage in not just antiwar protest, as in the 1960s, or the culture wars, as it was during the early

1990s, but in politics itself. And these developments, accelerated by an essentially televisual president who seeks to rule through meme-threats, are a reaction in part to knowledges articulated by both "intellectuals" and "activists." Even where the latter can be credited more than the former for having anticipated and made change, the lines are blurry; what appears in retrospect as haziness was two-way influence, and it mattered. Generations later, as Robin D. G. Kelley shows in his account of figures who were derided in the pre-Chomsky era as "premature anti-fascists," the dissenters have been revealed as truthtellers, even prophets of what was to come.



That is one reason why erasing history at the Smithsonian and the National Parks has become a bureaucratic priority. The lesson I take is that we will all have to be historians now, to remember that things were not always this way and to see through the growing morass of lies our government is propagating in public. There is no choice but to enter the breach, and we have to do it together. The biggest myth that intellectuals face, leading them to underestimate both their power and their responsibility, is the self-fulfilling sense that we work alone and for ourselves. We do not.

# On the Responsibility of Journalists

## *Jennifer Zacharia*

**In a recent series** of videos, Avichay Adraee, the Arabic-language spokesperson for the Israeli military, relentlessly attacked Anas al-Sharif, an *Al Jazeera* correspondent in northern Gaza. On July 20, while reporting on a particularly harrowing scene from the courtyard of al-Shifa Hospital, al-Sharif broke down emotionally when an emaciated woman collapsed from hunger beside him, as an ambulance arrived carrying some of the dozens of people killed by Israeli soldiers that day while waiting for bags of flour. Adraee accused him of shedding "crocodile tears." When al-Sharif called for a ceasefire, Adraee called him a "mouthpiece of intellectual terrorism."

To nearly all who watched him, al-Sharif's reporting has been nothing short of heroic and awe-inspiring. But to the Israeli government, he is culpable for having the audacity to document the starvation campaign it has engineered and imposed by brute force. It is not enough to enjoy the impunity afforded by U.S. and European cover: there should be no bad optics, either. Given the history of Israel's smearing of journalists in Gaza as a precursor to assassinating them, the Committee to Protect Journalists publicly called for al-Sharif's protection. But on August 10, an Israeli airstrike assassinated him and four other *Al Jazeera* journalists in a targeted attack on a tent outside al-Shifa Hospital.

Journalists, at their essence, epitomize the intellectual in Edward Said's telling, especially now when fascism plagues the country in which he lived and genocide threatens the existence of the people to whom he belonged. Said passed away twenty-two years ago, but he left us a trove of contemplations on what it means to live in exile and to be maligned and occluded in language and representation. He also probed the role of the intellectual in terrains plagued by violence, tumult, and catastrophe, often against the backdrop of stunted liberal understandings of peace.

In *Representations of the Intellectual*, his classic work from 1994, Said defined an intellectual as "an individual endowed with a faculty for representing, embodying, articulating a message, a view, an attitude, philosophy or opinion to, as well as for, a public"—what he called "a vocation for the art of representing." "This role," he continued,

> has an edge to it, and cannot be played without a sense of being someone whose place it is publicly to raise embarrassing questions, to confront orthodoxy and dogma (rather than to produce them), to be someone who cannot easily be co-opted by governments or corporations, and whose *raison d'être* is to represent all those people and issues that are routinely forgotten or swept under the rug. The intellectual does so on the basis of universal principles: that all human beings are entitled to expect decent standards of behavior

> concerning freedom and justice from worldly powers or nations, and that deliberate or inadvertent violations of these standards need to be testified and fought against courageously.

Said often spoke of the need for testimonials and facts to be recorded because, as he wrote, "human beings must create their own history." For no people is this more true than Palestinians. A robust archive of their existence, he felt, would counter the Israeli drive to silence and flatten it. Indeed, since the creation of the State of Israel, Palestinians have been construed as an inconvenient and breakable thorn in Israel's side, rather than an entire other people entitled to rights and aspirations. Instead of being allowed to articulate their own needs, desires, or liberation, Said explains, "Palestinians are expected to participate in the dismantling of their own history."



Thus when Said writes of the "vocation for the art of representing," he could have been speaking about Palestinian journalists. "Whether that is talking, writing, teaching, appearing on television," he writes, "that vocation is important to the extent that it is publicly recognizable and involves both commitment and risk, boldness and vulnerability."

Like al-Sharif, my cousin Shireen Abu Akleh, a journalist who worked tirelessly to bring attention to the unceasing wave of human rights violations against Palestinians, produced a collection of work that embodies Said's words. For that, on May 11, 2022, Shireen was shot and killed in Jenin by an Israeli soldier. Between 2000 and 2022, Israel killed at least twenty-six journalists and injured more than 300. Still, the assassination of Shireen was, at the time, notable; the killing of a high-profile, well-recognized figure, wearing a clearly marked press vest and helmet, was an especially egregious and attention-generating act even by Israeli standards.

I believe Israel intentionally killed Shireen, for three main reasons. One, she told the stories of Palestinians in their own words, thereby producing an ongoing record of Palestinian existence. Two, she provided Palestinians and other Arabs comfort and hope on both the bleakest and most ordinary days. And three, she was a voice that represented the unity and continuity of Palestinians across space and time.

Over three decades of reporting, Shireen created a narrative of Palestine and Palestinians. She consistently documented the contours of life under occupation—the excruciating details of imprisonments, killings, house demolitions, bombing campaigns—and she did so all while living in its midst. She spoke to the people who, in the West, had been relegated to largely nameless, faceless numbers and tagged with the label "terrorist" or "militant," rendering any subsequent detail or nuance irrelevant. But Shireen lived in those details, and she brought them to life.

Since her death, we've been told countless stories of what she meant to so many: those who met her once, those who knew her well, and those who saw her only on television. All reported their overwhelming sadness at her absence, her ability to make every person she interacted with feel seen and heard. In her telling of other people's stories, people recognized themselves and their neighbors, and in that, they found refuge. She told the truth—even when it was dangerous to do so—and documented the lives of people amid their suffering, as well as their more mundane moments. Journalists throughout Palestine, and especially in Gaza, have done the same: despite all odds, they have created a record of resilience and vulnerability, of love and community, in a time defined by cruelty, violence, and fragmentation.

The last twenty-two months have rewritten everything. Although Palestinian reporters have managed to narrate some stories of hope and return and reunions, the overwhelming reality is one of perpetual torment. Journalists have reported with courage and integrity under constant fire, knowing that they and their families could be targeted at any time. Unfortunately, Shireen's killing has also served as a harbinger of the onslaught against Palestinian journalists—in the last 662 days, Israel has killed 233 of them in Gaza.

And now, as bombs continue to fall and plans for ethnic cleansing are openly bandied about, there is the weaponization of starvation. On July 24, Agence France-Presse (AFP), the Associated Press, BBC, and Reuters issued an unprecedented statement expressing concern for journalists in Gaza who are being starved alongside their families and communities. The Society of Journalists at AFP stated that while they "have lost journalists in conflicts . . . none of us can ever remember seeing colleagues die of hunger." Meanwhile, a collection of Palestinian journalists—gaunt and nearly unrecognizable from their images of two years ago—are on the eleventh day of hunger strike, which will not end, they say, until every child in Gaza has access to food and water. Still, these reporters and their colleagues continue to rush toward buildings just hit by air strikes, searching for survivors, looking to document the losses and the crimes. When al-Sharif began crying that heartbreaking day in front of al-Shifa Hospital, you could hear the people around him comforting and encouraging him: "Continue! Continue! You're our voice."

What is the role of intellectuals when the erasure of words is matched by the erasure of bodies? During a genocide, everything takes on new significance. Palestinian writers, journalists, and poets have demonstrated the urgency of creating meaning while faced with existential precarity. Palestinian educators, and artists also do this work, as do the health care providers, rescue workers, and civil defenders who hold press conferences, conduct interviews, and insist on remaining in besieged hospitals despite the risk, their very presence a testament to the ongoing horrors.

Palestinians facing extermination navigate language and insist on survival and representation. Alaa Alqaisi, a Palestinian writer in Gaza, has recently shed light on the importance of documenting one's experiences despite the increasing difficulty of doing so in the face of starvation:

> It is not a matter of forgetfulness but erosion, a steady unraveling of everything I believed belonged to me. And yet I persist. I speak. I write. Because silence would be a deeper form of defeat. Testimony, even if cracked and uncertain, is the only offering I can still give. To keep it locked inside would be to let this hunger consume even the voice that names it.

Although Said is not with us today to inveigh against the genocide of his people, he left us with this prophetic framing: "The major choice faced by the intellectual is whether to be allied with the stability of the victors and rulers, or—the more difficult path—to consider that stability as a state of emergency threatening the less fortunate, the experience of subordination itself, the memory of forgotten voices and persons, with the danger of complete extinction."

# On the Responsibility of Citizens

## *Martin O'Neill*





**"AN INDIVIDUAL** then has choices," Noam Chomsky wrote in these pages on the tenth anniversary of September 11. Consider, in this regard, the story of two remarkable women recently arrested in Britain.

In early July, Reverend Sue Parfitt, age eighty-three, was arrested in Parliament Square in London. A retired priest and former social worker and family therapist, she was sitting on a camping chair, holding a sign: "I oppose genocide. I support Palestine Action." For this quiet act of peaceful protest, Parfitt was arrested under powers granted to the British police under the 2000 Terrorism Act, following a vote by Parliament in early July to add Palestine Action to a list of proscribed terrorist organizations. In reality, the group is no more than a political protest network, founded in 2020 to engage in acts of civil disobedience and nonviolent direct action.

One suspects that Parfitt will take this encounter in her stride, given that she has been arrested over two dozen times for similar acts of protest and civil disobedience. She is driven by a deep Christian faith that puts her fundamentally at odds with the standards for restricting political protest and political speech that the British state, under the current Labour government, would hope to impose on her. "Life is about radical obedience to the will of God," she has said, and her prayer and reflection have brought her to the view that God's will is that people should do what they can to protect the lives of their fellow human beings and to protect the planet for future generations. "I acted out of love," she stated after a previous arrest for protesting inaction on climate change. She did so again in July, even though that choice puts her directly at odds with the power of the state. As she said moments before her arrest, "I know that we are in the right place doing the right thing."

Audrey White comes from a different tradition than Parfitt, but the depth and clarity of their moral commitments have something in common. White first came to prominence in the 1980s when she led a union campaign against sexual harassment in the workplace. The manager of a local branch of a clothing store in Liverpool, she was told by four of her staff that an area manager had been making unwanted sexual advances toward them. She complained on their behalf and was fired. When White refused to accept this outcome and turned up at work anyway, her superiors threatened to call the police to have her removed. Her response was to start a picket of the store. Given that—as White herself puts it—"no one crosses a picket-line in Liverpool," this turned out to be an effective tactic. She was supported by "dockers, car workers, staff from unemployed centres, union members, local activists." Further pickets were organized for the firm's London and Manchester stores. Management ultimately relented, and White was reinstated.

By engaging in this kind of political action, White and her comrades were breaching the ban on secondary picketing that had been brought in by the Thatcher government's 1980 Employment Act. But they were also doing what they believed to be right, on a point of fundamental principle. Their actions changed the climate on sexual harassment at work, striking a blow for workers' rights and gender equality. Today White is held up by the Trades Union Congress as one of 150 standout examples of campaigners who have changed things for the better for working people over the past 150 years in the United Kingdom. Her story was made into a 1987 film, *Business as Usual*, starring Glenda Jackson in Audrey's role.

White's formidable capacity to stand up to bullies, and to be guided by doing what is right rather than taking the easy road in the face of injustice, has not faded. Just two weeks after Parfitt's arrest, White was again in Liverpool's city center, holding up a sign, and standing up for simple truths. Her sign, like Parfitt's, proclaimed a simple message, "I oppose genocide and occupation. I support Palestine Action." Unlike Parfitt, though, when the Merseyside Police came to arrest her for this "terrorist offense," she did not allow herself to be led away. Instead, she just stayed put and had to be dragged off by four police officers. Onlookers shouted at the police, "Shame on you!" White has a heart condition and low bone density, but she put herself on the line because she saw the simple truth of the moral horror being perpetrated by the government of Israel against the people of Gaza.

As Robin D. G. Kelley notes in his essay in this issue, Chomsky's 1967 essay on "The Responsibility of Intellectuals" was inspired by

Dwight Macdonald's reflection under the same title, originally published in 1945. Macdonald ended with the simple conclusion, "It is a great thing to be able to see what is right under your nose." Sue Parfitt and Audrey White both see something that is right under our noses. And like the men and women whom Kelley spotlights for standing up to fascism, they have both made their choices.

The simple truth is that the British government continues to be complicit in the genocidal crimes against humanity being perpetrated by Israeli armed forces in Gaza. The government continues to sell arms to Israel, and the Royal Air Force, from its Akrotiri base in Cyprus, continues to collaborate on intelligence gathering for the IDF. Prime Minister Keir Starmer has said that Israel "has the right" to cut off power and water to Gaza, and Foreign Secretary David Lammy told the House of Commons in September last year that "I am very comfortable with the support we give to Israel." (He may yet have good reason to be less comfortable: as Conservative MP Kit Malthouse told Lammy in the House of Commons in late July, Lammy "may end up at The Hague" due to his "inaction—and frankly, cowardice.")

In the face of these conditions, as the Israeli government's genocidal actions continue in Gaza and notionally liberal democratic countries turn toward repression and authoritarianism, I share Kelley's assessment that the terms of debate we inherit from Macdonald and Chomsky feel misplaced and anachronistic. Knowledge of both genocide abroad and repression at home has been democratized. Thanks to the internet, the facts are really under all our noses and available to everyone—accessible just as much to retired priests and retired shopworkers as they are to those who work in universities. And as Kelley observes, universities on both sides of the Atlantic are no longer sites of "privilege" when it comes to intellectual freedom and freedom from the pressures of the market and the state, the university system having come under systematic attack.

But the cases of Parfitt and White reveal still more. They show that we miss something essential when we frame our talk of responsibilities around "intellectuals," as opposed to the responsibilities of all citizens. Political responsibility is a predominantly moral rather than intellectual affair. There is no need for abstruse theory, complex intellectual analysis, or insider information to know what is wrong with the murder of the innocent, to know what is wrong when the state represses its own people, to know what is wrong with the silencing of dissent. Politicians such as Starmer and Lammy—with postgraduate law degrees from Oxford and Harvard, respectively—have been trained in international law and human rights; their failings are not intellectual failings, a matter of imperfectly applied expertise, but grotesque, disfiguring *moral* failings. To critique their disgraceful actions, ordinary citizens only need to be able to speak the simple truth.

Allow me a further example. As Home Secretary, Yvette Cooper will go down in history for betraying British traditions of free speech and political contestation. She has used the power of legal sanctions and the blunt tool of physical force by police to restrict protest and dissent, undermining the most fundamental requirements of a liberal democratic society. But again this does not stem from ignorance, nor can it be traced to a chiefly intellectual defect. Cooper took a first class degree in Philosophy, Politics and Economics from Balliol College, Oxford. During her studies, she would have read J. S. Mill and Isaiah Berlin on liberty, Ronald Dworkin and Joseph Raz on rights, John Rawls on Martin Luther King, Jr. and the place of civil disobedience in a democratic society. Cooper is at home in the world of ideas and knows what she is doing.

Authoritarian politicians such as Cooper, Lammy, and Starmer are, indeed, in many ways members of an intellectual elite. They act as they do because, although they understand the core values of freedom and democracy, and understand the significance of international law and human rights, they are quite content to exercise the power of their office in a way that dishonors those values. Their failings are not intellectual failings, but moral failings—that is the simple fact under our nose.

Those of us who live under governments like Britain's today are faced with a world where many of our politicians are intellectually adept but cowardly, self-serving, and morally bankrupt. Yet a democratic public committed to the basic principles of freedom and equality will not be harried into docility and conformity by the crude tools of authoritarian repression. Hope lies in the ways that people from a huge variety of backgrounds and walks of life have realized that, whatever the politicians do, individuals have choices, including the choice to call things as they are, both in factual and in moral terms. Ordinary resistance and ordinary responsibility—including the responsibility "to speak the truth and to expose lies"—falls on all of us, whatever our jobs, positions, or roles in society.

Where I live in York, one of our local bakers, the Haxby Bakehouse, has been notably outspoken on social media in condemning the genocide in Gaza and expressing solidarity with Palestine. I wrote to say how much I appreciated their use of their voice and their platform. They replied, "We saw a social media post that said 'if your favourite band aren't saying free Palestine, then you need a new favourite band,' maybe we should change *band* for *bakery*." Their words contain an urgent lesson: whoever we are and whatever we do for a living, as democratic citizens we must always speak the truth to others as we see it and refuse to be silent in the face of inhumanity and injustice. **BR**

Image: Getty Images

# THE MAMDANI MODEL

## How to save a party in free fall.

*David Austin Walsh*

THE DEMOCRATIC PARTY is in crisis. The party's popularity numbers are abysmal: a March poll by NBC News found that only 27 percent of registered voters have positive views of the Democrats, the lowest since the poll began in 1990, and things have only declined since then. Other polls have found that the approval rating of congressional Democrats is underwater even among Democratic voters, with only around a third expressing satisfaction with the Democrats' performance on Capitol Hill. Senate Minority Leader Chuck Schumer's approval rating, in particular, is hovering around 17 percent. (Nearly 80 percent of Republicans, by contrast, approve of the congressional GOP.) Even big donors are beginning to tighten their purse-strings.

And then there's Zohran Mamdani. His decisive victory in the New York mayoral primary against establishment sex pest Andrew Cuomo, the former-governor-son-of-a-former-governor, underlines how Democrats have arrived at something like their own Tea Party moment: voters fed up with the feckless, corrupt dealings and nepotism of a hollowed-out Democratic Party registered their dissatisfaction in the highest-profile race of 2025, despite a torrent of national criticism and propaganda from the establishment (and a mountain of funding for Cuomo). Though he faces a serious hurdle in the general election this fall, there is a good chance that a thirty-three-year-old pro-Palestinian, Muslim, democratic socialist will displace Eric Adams to become the next mayor of the largest city in the country.



How did we get here? Democratic voters are disgusted with the party's leadership for failing to live up to their own words last year, when senior Democrats called Trump a fascist and threat to American democracy. Those Democrats were right, as the deployment of National Guardsmen and active-duty Marines to Los Angeles to quell largely peaceful anti-ICE protests in June only further confirms. But while masked, heavily armed, unidentified men are grabbing people off the streets and federal agents are throwing Democratic senators to the ground for attending news conferences, those same senior leaders are either offering milquetoast statements (Schumer: "we need immediate answers to what the hell went on"), proclaiming vague nothings (Obama: "now is precisely the time to ask ourselves tough questions about how we can build our democracies"), feeding the anti-Mamdani machine (Hakeem Jeffries), or hawking a book (Kamala Harris). The left, meanwhile, remains furious over the establishment's support for the Gaza genocide, and the party is still reeling from Joe Biden's catastrophic decision to run for re-election.

Part of the problem is that there is little consensus about what exactly the Democratic Party stands for in policy terms beyond unconditional support for Israel, some attention to climate change, and vaguely defined commitments to racial, gender, and sexual equity (never mind the sexual harassment allegations against Cuomo). Any positive vision for the Democratic Party should certainly include the expansion of the state's capacity to do things, and liberal pundits Ezra Klein and Derek Thompson have attempted to lay out a more affirmative agenda—"abundance"—in their recent book by that title. But as Sandeep Vaheesan argues in these pages, Klein and Thompson's thinking remains structured in many ways by neoliberalism, and anyway much of the actually existing political muscle for the "abundance agenda" is astroturfed from wealthy Silicon Valley donors.



**While masked men are grabbing people off the streets, senior Democrats are proclaiming vague nothings or feeding the anti-Mamdani machine.**

Perhaps this is the reason that abundance featured so prominently at WelcomeFest, the self-described "largest public gathering of centrist Democrats" that took place early in June. Speakers included Andrew Rotherham, a major nonprofit leader who reprimanded Florida Democrats for opposing Ron DeSantis's "Don't Say Gay" bill; blogger and Biden White House whisperer Matthew Yglesias, who blamed "The Groups"—his favored term for progressive advocacy organizations—for the Democrats' electoral woes; and economist Josh Barro, who said point-blank in an interview with New York congressman Ritchie Torres that "when I look at policies in New York that stand in the way of abundance . . . if you look under the hood, you eventually find a labor union at the end."

Another key factor behind the failure of the Democratic establishment is that it once again proved incapable of accommodating internal reform. Twenty-five-year-old liberal activist David Hogg, elected as one of five vice-chairs of the Democratic National Committee (DNC) in February, said he would not run again after a vote to hold new vice-chair elections on procedural grounds passed with an overwhelming majority in early June.

The trouble started in April when Hogg announced plans to use his PAC, Leaders We Deserve, to support primary challenges by young progressives against "out-of-touch, ineffective" Democrats in safe blue congressional districts. Hogg's initiative was one of the first serious programs within the Democratic Party apparatus to take this problem seriously. DNC chair Ken Martin disputes that the bid for new vice-chair elections was retaliation for Hogg's attacks on complacent incumbents. But *come on.*

Though the original procedural complaint was filed in February, a DNC panel recommended a re-do in May, after Hogg had gone on the offensive; it beggars belief that the body-wide tally had nothing to do with his criticism of the party. In a conversation leaked to *Politico*, Martin complained that Hogg's attacks "essentially destroyed any chance I have" to successfully assert his leadership and raise money.

Until quite recently, Hogg had few trappings of anti-establishment political radicalism. He rose to national prominence as a high school student after speaking out about the February 2018 Parkland school shooting, soon becoming the face of progressive gun-control activism. A month later he served as a co-organizer of the March for Our Lives protests, an outgrowth of the left-liberal protest energy of the Women's March the previous year. He was featured, alongside his fellow student organizers, on the cover of *Time* and was included in the magazine's list of the 100 most influential people of the year. He wrote a bestselling book about the shooting and student organizing, tweeted out views like "I love capitalism," and enrolled at Harvard in 2019.

In short, Hogg was extremely well positioned for a career in mainstream Democratic politics of just the sort on display at WelcomeFest. And indeed, until his launch of Leaders We Deserve, he had never offered serious criticism of the party or its leadership beyond criticizing the records of some Democrats on gun control. Instead, he dismissed left-wing critiques of the party's corruption by corporate cash and declined to endorse Bernie Sanders or Elizabeth Warren in the 2020 primary. Since stepping down as vice-chair he has indeed moved to the left, including by endorsing Mamdani, but his PAC still makes no mention of substantive reform proposals beyond running younger people.

Why, then, did Liam Kerr, a cofounder of the PAC that hosts WelcomeFest, go scorched-earth against Hogg on his Substack in February this year, well before the showdown inside the DNC?

---

**THE ANSWER** is a classic case of what philosopher Olúfẹ́mi O. Táíwò has called "deference politics," though operating in a way many people fail to recognize.

The phenomenon evolved out of a certain strain of left-wing organizing practices in the 2010s but soon spread to predominantly liberal, mainstream spaces where ideas like "progressive stacks" and "centering" people who belong to marginalized groups flourished. In its strongest form, Táíwò notes, deference politics not only encourages passing the mic to representatives of oppressed communities. It also promotes a culture where criticizing the views of such representatives draws reflexive suspicion—interpreted as a sign of wayward refusal to defer to those who know better. And, because the people who populate influential advocacy organizations and the halls of power are rarely the typical member of the groups they purport to speak for, deference politics in these settings easily falls prey to "elite capture," "the control over political agendas and resources by a group's most advantaged people."

In developing this critique, Táíwò was taking aim at what he called "being-in-the-room privilege." The point was to remind us of all those people *excluded* from the rooms where the most consequential social and political decisions get made. In a striking twist, however, self-identified centrists and moderates in the Democratic Party have adapted a similar-sounding critique to decry the supposed iron grip of the "woke" left. According to critics of "The Groups" like Yglesias, Klein, Adam Jentleson, and Ruy Teixeira, deference is the primary source of the party's problems because, they say, it gives marginal, radical activists a platform for talking in unpopular ways or extracting unpopular policy concessions. Either way, the complaint goes, the effect is to alienate majorities and trash the Democratic brand.

What does this have to do with Hogg? Young middle-class white men are hardly a marginalized group in American life, of course, but Hogg is also a survivor of gun violence, and he did plausibly benefit from some degree of deference on those grounds as a young activist. That is exactly what Kerr found objectionable in February: the moral authority that Hogg had accrued on this issue won him a big audience, which he used to attack the records of moderate Democrats on gun control. (Never mind that a large supermajority of Democratic voters favor tougher gun laws.)

The irony is that deference really is the source of the Democratic Party's woes, but not in the way these critics say. Shallow forms of identity-based deference, especially in online spaces, have become familiar over the last five years, but whatever objections one might reasonably raise against them, the argument that woke "Groups" are primarily responsible for tanking the Democratic brand mistakes where power really lies. The most damaging and consequential form of deference politics is the form practiced by the moderate, milquetoast, legacy establishment itself—the establishment that relentlessly impugns critics, disdains efforts to deepen democracy in the party, and demands deference to its own authority, hierarchy, and power, often through the very identity-based appeals that "Groups" critics associate with insurgent radicals. This is exactly the kind of deference that Táíwò was criticizing, and its effect is to reinforce the problem of elite impunity among the leaders, pollsters, and consultants who have run the party into the ground.

Of course, elite deference has suffused Democratic politics for a very long time, but over the last decade it has only intensified in reaction to an ever more viable challenge from the populist left. In 2014, amid calls for Ruth Bader Ginsburg to retire so that a liberal seat on the Court might be preserved, defenders insisted that her critics were being sexist, ageist, and ungrateful—a line that did not age well after her death and replacement by Amy Coney Barrett, one of the key votes in the *Dobbs* decision overturning *Roe v. Wade*. So went a similar rationale for Hillary Clinton's 2016 presidential bid: after Obama's presidency, it was now a woman's turn. The left's antipathy for her candidacy was dismissed first as the misogyny of "Bernie Bros" and then as racism, a refusal to listen to Black voters in the primaries. And then, in 2020, concerns about Biden's age and fitness for the presidency were brushed aside—even by people who raised similar concerns about Sanders—again on the grounds of ageism.

The controversy ignited by the publication of Jake Tapper and Alex Thompson's recent book *Original Sin*, a classic political gossip journalism vivisection of Biden's decision to run for a second term, underscores the point. If the revelations are to be believed, then the Democratic Party—really the liberal establishment writ large—engaged in a deliberate conspiracy to conceal, downplay, and dismiss the extent of Biden's mental and physical incapacitation, culminating in his disastrous debate performance against Trump in June 2024. This is a scandal of the gravest possible seriousness, one that indicts not just Biden himself but his family, his close advisors, senior Democratic Party leaders, and many media figures, including Tapper and Thompson themselves. (Like many prominent journalists, they evidently chose to sit on a crucial political story until *after* the election in order to sell books.)

The book also exposes the Democratic Party's narratives about Trump—that he is morally and mentally unfit for office and a narcissistic liar—as fundamentally hollow. According to Tapper and Thompson, Biden was mentally unfit for office, could not come to terms with his diminishment due to his narcissism, and actively misled the public until it was too late. And because contemporary liberal political culture demands deference to power, authority, and the ideals of technocratic competence and meritocracy—as one of Biden's staffers infamously put it, the president was "just that fucking good"—there was no serious challenge to Biden's authority until his debate performance finally mobilized elite Democrats against him. And even then, Biden stayed in the race for nearly a month!



**Mamdani's dramatic upset shows the path forward: a big-tent grassroots organization that speaks to the needs of all voters fed up with a sclerotic party establishment.**

Political scientists Daniel Schlozman and Sam Rosenfeld argue that both the Democratic and Republican parties have been hollowed out: "organizationally top-heavy and poorly rooted" and "dominated by satellite groups," they now "command little respect in the eyes of voters and activists alike." The GOP has been "pulled to radicalism," they claim, by the "committed actors" of the American conservative movement, culminating in Trump's cult of personality. The Democrats, meanwhile, have been "rendered listless by conflicting actors"—the challenges inherent in reconciling historically working-class commitments with the rise of new and powerful professional and corporate constituencies.

What this misses is that Democrats are also beset by personality cults—indeed, they are a key aspect of elite deference. Just consider the enduring reverence for Obama, whose presidency accelerated the hollowing out of the party and culminated in the election of Trump—but who, like Harris, has now basically renounced any place on the national stage as the country slides more and more into authoritarianism. The Democratic

Party infrastructure serves less as a mode of governance for a party committed to contesting political power and more as a spoils system for the consultant class no matter whether they help candidates win or lose.

---



**Where should we expect** things to go from here? Hogg's purge may seem to confirm a hard limit to internal reformism. Sanders's supporters and the broader field of democratic socialists already learned as much when they contested various party leadership positions and internal rules changes under the first Trump administration—a campaign that was only partially successful. The AIPAC-fueled unseating of Squad members Cori Bush and Jamaal Bowman likewise portends limited room for messaging change on Israel.

And yet, the crisis has reached such proportions now that possibilities may be more open than in the past. The last DNC chair, Jaime Harrison, owed his position to nepotism and favor-trading—he was a protégé of South Carolina party boss Jim Clyburn, who essentially served as kingmaker in the 2020 primary. Though he failed to stand up for Hogg, Martin formerly served as chair of the Minnesota Democratic-Farmer-Labor Party, which has dominated Minnesota state politics for the past generation in spite of the Upper Midwest's red shift. He has pledged to shore up the party's relationship with organized labor and set the party back on a fifty-state strategy, reversing the increasingly obsessive focus on messaging to swing-state voters.

This vision for the party is generally at odds with the vision voiced at WelcomeFest. The Abundists are a well-organized and well-financed faction of the Democratic coalition, seeking to reassert megadonor- and Silicon Valley–friendly politics over the party. In other words, they are the faction of elite deference politics. The primary competing vision is left-wing populism: a politics centered on grassroots political mobilization, skepticism of large donors and Big Tech and other corporate monopolies, explicit demands for higher taxation of the wealthy, and a robust commitment to public goods in health care, education, and housing. Sanders, Alexandria Ocasio-Cortez, and now Mamdani are the public faces of this formation.

Hogg tried to leverage the ambiguous legacy of liberal activist culture during the first Trump administration, pursuing social and cultural capital within the party establishment. He hit a dead end, but he learned his lesson. He endorsed Mamdani. And as Mamdani's dramatic upset makes clear, his strategy represents the path forward for Democrats and the left: a robust, big-tent grassroots political organization that incorporates the populism rather than shutting it out and speaks to the needs of all voters ill-served by and fed up with a sclerotic party establishment.

It's about damn time. **BR**

# BUILDING A POLITICAL HOME



## *Cathy J. Cohen in conversation with Brandon M. Terry*

*CATHY J. COHEN IS one of the most distinguished political scientists in the American academy. Over the course of her career, she has dramatically reshaped how many of us think about questions of inequality, stigma, and marginalization in American politics and pierced through unexamined assumptions about how Americans, especially youth, approach major questions of political life. Influenced by traditions of Black radical feminism, she is especially celebrated—as well as criticized—for her sharp critiques of mainstream Black and gay civil rights organizations, as well as the paradigms through which they are studied. While many scholars sought influence through more familiar venues of public intellectualism, Cohen quietly impacted successive generations of activists, organizers, students, and civic leaders in Chicago and elsewhere with her ideas and mentorship, especially in the early days of Black Lives Matter.*

*After a period where it seemed that many of the ideas and organizations she championed were ascendant, such efforts now face a wave of hostility and derision, as reactionary political forces elicit and extend outrage against the supposed excesses of the gains won by Blacks, immigrants, leftists, queer folks, and others. On July 3, I spoke with Cohen about the attacks on progressivism, what makes social movements work, and the challenge of the second coming of Trumpism.*

*—Brandon M. Terry*

**BRANDON TERRY:** As I speak, Congress has passed Donald Trump's so-called Big Beautiful Bill, which some commentators consider one of the most consequential single pieces of legislation ever passed. And I think it also represents—alongside the dismantling of civil rights legislation and attacks on higher education—the larger ideological and political ambitions of the second Trump administration. How do you think Black politics ought to respond?

**CATHY COHEN:** We are in the midst of a fight like none we've ever seen before in our lifetimes. And there's no denying the fundamental role of white supremacy, racial capitalism, and Christian nationalism in structuring Trump's attacks on Black and Brown people through this second term. The first round of this terror has come in the form of what we might call "anti-wokeism," with the explicit goal of dismantling all things thought to be related to extending opportunity and possibly advancement to folks of color and fundamentally shifting power in this country. The right is using this anti-woke framework to explain away everything they contend is wrong with the country, from the problems at "elite universities" to the stunning claim that DEI caused a plane crash.

The attacks on DEI both target and represent Black and Brown folks as incompetent workers who, they say, have been given an advantage over white people by the government. We have to understand the expansive nature of this work: anti-wokeism is about giving ideological cover to longstanding priorities on the right—dismantling the welfare state and ramping up the carceral state, especially in the form of immigrant deportation and detention on the streets at home and militarism overseas.

**BT:** What is jarring to me is that we've lived through an explosion in popular education about race, especially in the last fifteen years. When I was in college, a graduate student advised me, "Whatever you do, don't work on residential segregation. No one will want to hear about it." Today many educated people know what redlining is. How could we have lived through this proliferation of interventions about the history of racial injustice and yet are also seeing this revived story of Black incompetence?

**CC:** We have to understand that many of Trump's attacks are not "culture wars" as described in the media, but a *generational* war meant to win over, in particular, young white people. The success of our research, writing, and teaching the truthful narrative of the history of racism, empire, and white supremacy in this country is changing the way young people—and especially white people— think about institutions, about their role in society, about white privilege and racial capitalism. This has been especially true for young people with some access to college.

However, for non-college-educated young white people—who have experienced an increasing vulnerability and precarity and declining access to the white privilege and state power they were told was theirs for the taking, even from their class position—this has built resentment around what is narrated as the unworthy advantages of communities of color, through policies like affirmative action or the expansion of the state for the social and economic mobility of, in particular, the Black middle class. Trump's message to these young white people is that they have to stop this transgenerational transformation. And part of stopping it is controlling the university, controlling public education—taking back control of the narrative of this country and about people of color and promoting an explanation that white people have less because people of color have more. These two things are deeply influencing each other.

**BT:** But how do you explain the Trump movement's appeal to so many Americans who would not understand themselves to be white? There was a lot of movement among Latino voters—Latino male voters in particular—with some movement among a very small segment of Black men, including high-profile online influencers like DJ Akademiks. If this is about white supremacy, why do we see this complex racial demographic mix-up?

**CC:** The broad agenda of the MAGA movement and the Trump administration is not just about white supremacy; it is also about Christian nationalism. Part of what Trump promises is that men will take what patriarchy tells us is their rightful place as the head of their family. So, even if they don't have access to economic mobility, men are promised access to patriarchal power. And for men of color with limited access to the spoils of capitalism, he's even offering new kinds of financial systems such as cryptocurrency.

My research project, the GenForward Survey, conducted focus groups with young Black men about Trump during the campaign. Our participants had an instrumental view of their possible support of Trump, and this has everything to do with the absence of deliverables from the left to those communities. Many of the young men we talked to had no illusions that Trump was on their side or would truly make their lives better. But they didn't believe that Biden was on their side, either. What they believed was that Trump would at least try to pay them off: the last time Trump was in office, they got a check, and many of them noted they didn't get that from Biden.

**"I never have the expectation that all Black people will line up together. My view is built around meaningful political solidarity, not just identity-based solidarity."**

When we said to the participants in the focus group, "Well, Trump lies," they said, "Everybody lies—this whole political system is built on lies." And then when we said, "Well, what about the idea that Trump is racist?" they said, "They're all racist. He just says what they think." These young men had a deep—and I think appropriate—skepticism about the inherent racism of both political parties.

The young men considered voting for Trump because they believed they might get some symbolic representation or some minor policy wins that would temporarily enhance their lives. I'm not saying I agree with them, but they articulated a position that they'd rather go with the guy who gave them money, who's trying to buy them off, and who performs a certain type of masculinity that maybe they aspire to. We know what Trump's play is. The question is, what is the left offering these same young Black men? The gender politics of Trump's Christian nationalism might be enticing for groups of racially and economically marginalized young men who feel like they don't have access to power in a society that says men are supposed to.

**BT:** But even on the most charitable interpretation, Trump's relationship to religion seems thin and instrumental, not deeply committed.

Why does the Christian right see him as a vehicle for the restoration of a "postliberal" Christian era?

**CC:** He's advancing their agenda. That's the reality. He gave them *Dobbs*, which will then facilitate the mobilization at some point, maybe after the midterm elections, of a federal national ban on abortion. He has reinstated the centrality of the nuclear family and the heteropatriarchal roles in that family. He's taking on gender nonconformity and destroying all the protections and services won by and for transgender communities. He is embracing the agenda of many white Christian nationalist churches, in particular. Would they prefer a person who articulated and lived their ideology exactly? Sure. But they can live with someone who's going to deliver wins for them. Because in the end, the idea is to accumulate power so that you can transform and control institutions to advance your political agenda. It's not complicated.

I think most people understand the pay-to-play relationship that surrounds evangelicals, for example, and their support of Trump. That has caused some fracture in those communities. But yesterday I heard an interview with a congressmember, House Freedom Caucus Chair Andy Harris, about the "big ugly bill" that I found revealing. When asked if he was "caving" by voting for the bill despite his concerns about its impact on the deficit, he replied: "Well, if winning is caving, then I guess we caved." There you go.

**BT:** Your first book, *The Boundaries of Blackness: AIDS and the Breakdown of Black Politics*, gave such a sophisticated, empirically grounded theory of the cleavages within Black political life and the ways that they leave certain segments of the larger group marginalized, even in times of great emergency like the HIV crisis. You've been working on that theme since then: Black people disagree. They have deep conflicts. Their solidarity is fragile and contingent. It needs certain conditions to thrive, and may have objectionable consequences at times. But every election cycle, we continuously go through the ritual of being surprised by this. Why do you think your message is so hard for public commentators to digest?

**CC:** *Boundaries* was a case study about the politics of HIV and AIDS in Black communities, but it was really intended to help us think about who has power, legitimacy, voice, and resources in terms of defining "a" Black political agenda—even in, or especially in, life-and-death circumstances.

There are many people—W. E. B. Du Bois, Manning Marable, Angela Davis, Michael Dawson—who've written about the complexities and different ideological positions of Black people and communities. Many Black feminists have done this as well. Why do public commentators seem to miss this point? There are a couple reasons. The narratives of our diversity, our different positionalities, our different politics are sometimes in tension with what might be considered the unifying themes of Black solidarity that arise in response to a form of anti-Blackness and structural racism that negates the basic humanity of Black people. If I'm trying to respond to arguments about the dehumanization of Black people, I'm not going to focus on the very real differences in Black experiences and positionality—I'm going to make a unifying argument about our humanity.

Another reason is the way scholarship on Blackness is framed and considered relative to other groups. This is typical in political science: researchers often ask how Black people compare to white people, or how Black women compare to white women. But that framework of comparison flattens the specificity of Black experiences and Black politics. Sadly, this comparative approach defines far too much academic work, particularly in the social sciences and biological sciences.

We need a deeper understanding of the dynamics of Black communities, because we can never effectively represent and organize Black people without that. You can't understand the carceral state and its targeting of Black communities without attention to gender, as extraordinary work by scholars such as Beth Richie and Sarah Haley has shown. Premilla Nadasen adds depth to our understanding of class politics in Black communities by detailing how poor Black women built movements of resistance to the contraction of the welfare state. C. Riley Snorton, Jafari Allen, Moya Bailey, and E. Patrick Johnson help us understand the intersections between gender, sexuality, and race and transgender politics in Black communities. I could go on and on highlighting more extraordinary work. The point is that all this scholarship is informing and advancing liberatory formations while paying attention to differential lived experiences and political positionings of Black people.

**BT:** Is there a place for Black solidarity going forward, then? Does the complexity of Black experiences still allow us to use that language, or is it time for a new vocabulary?

**CC:** I'm not invested in some magical, expansive Black solidarity that's built around our lowest common denominator. Instead, I am committed to a Black solidarity that is built, as bell hooks would tell us, "from margin to center," around our political commitments and liberatory vision. I am working to build a Black solidarity that includes and centers transgender Black people, Black women and gender non-conforming folks, poor and working-class Black people, disabled Black people. But here is the other dimension: we also have to think about a political formation of solidarity that extends beyond that Black community that includes all those with a shared commitment to fighting oppression in its many dimensions—and that includes, yes, some white people.

While I'm deeply committed to a solidarity that centers continuous resistance to anti-Blackness and structural racism, we have to think about how we can build an expansive and transformative kind of solidarity. I am rejecting a limited or traditional form of Black solidarity, which is often embedded in the ways people talk about institutions like the NAACP. I'm working to build a left Black solidarity that's prepared to fight the emerging fascism taking root in this country and that's built around *some* Black people and *some* Black communities. I never have the expectation that all Black people will line up together: my work around HIV/AIDS and my life coming from a working-class family and as a Black lesbian feminist has made that clear. My view of solidarity is built around meaningful political solidarity, not just identity-based solidarity.

**BT:** Zohran Mamdani just won a surprise upset over Andrew Cuomo in the New York Democratic primary. That has set the stage for what looks like a contentious general election between Eric Adams—who comes out of his own Black institutional and associational life in Reverend Herb Daughtry's church and the nationalist organizing that was going on there—and Mamdani, whose politics, I think, are closer to yours (not to mention an independent Cuomo and the conservative Curtis Sliwa).

Mamdani has pretty weak Black support, except when you zero in on young people and the self-described Black left.

You know something about these splits from your other career mentoring and supporting Black youth activists who work at a local level in Chicago with Black Youth Project 100 (BYP100). Since 2012 you've played an important role, giving them institutional resources and moral and intellectual support as well as helping people think about these complexities and try to put them into practice. How have you seen Black youth political engagement evolve, particularly across gender and generational lines?



**CC:** BYP100 emerged because of brilliant young activists. I was lucky to be able to watch and support their amazing work—for instance, holding police accountable for the killing of young Black people like Rekia Boyd and Laquan McDonald. They also offered a new framing of the history of neoliberal disinvestment in Black communities through the call to divest from the carceral state and invest in Black and other resource-marginalized communities.

But even though we talked earlier in the interview about generational differences, I'm always a little careful with that frame. There are real differences *within* generations that we can't lose sight of. So when we talk about how generational politics have changed over time, I always like to remind people that the politics of young adults evolve most often in relation to the social and political context they encounter. Millennials and members of Gen Z, for example, have lived through the recessions of 2008, recessions related to COVID, and the impending recession that may come from Trump's tariffs. In some ways they have had more opportunity than previous generations, but they have also had to take on more debt to access promised educational opportunity. They're less likely to own a home at this point in their life cycle than other generations. These are young people who have experienced a neoliberal, multiracial politics that culminated in the election of the first Black president—an election that also helped to facilitate the election of Trump and his white, Christian nationalist agenda. They are much more skeptical of state-run institutions, even what we might call democratic institutions, than other generations. They largely don't believe in the two-party system: they want a third party. And when we ask them in our GenForward surveys about the best way to make change in the country, they don't say elections. They say organizing, activism, nonviolent protests, and even civic engagement. When we ask young Black people the best way to make racial progress, again, they don't mention traditional forms of politics. One out of five say revolution.

**"There is a tension between creating institutions that feel safe and moving beyond them to do the work of movement building."**

These young people don't believe that incremental change through traditional political institutions will ever deliver the transformational agenda that they embrace. This viewpoint has moved some to embrace social movement formations calling for radical transformative change. But for others, there is deep cynicism about the effectiveness of collective mobilization, which causes them to lean instead toward an individualized politics, often using social media platforms to register their preferences. And still for others, their skepticism has promoted the idea of distrust in any kind of institution, fostering a belief that they must provide for each other outside traditional institutions with practices that might be labeled mutual aid.

**BT:** There seems to be a widespread sense that the Black Lives Matter movement is essentially over—or if not over, then in decisive retreat, maybe even defeat. Do you agree, and if so, what are the chief causes of the movement's decline?

**CC:** I participate in social movements, and I also study them. And that has taught me these lessons: first, movements are never steady and linear. We need ways of assessing the work of movements when their work is fever-pitched—what happened around Ferguson or the mass mobilizations of 2020. And we also must be able to assess work that happens in movement spaces when they appear more dormant. We are not currently seeing the same activity from movements that we witnessed in opposition to the killings of Trayvon Martin, Michael Brown, Breonna Taylor, and George Floyd, but there's still activity among organizations such as BYP100, Dream Defenders, the Movement for Black Lives, and the Rising

Majority. All of these organizations are helping to analyze this moment and to build and maintain the spaces and campaigns meant to organize communities into resistance.

The second lesson is that social movements and their organizations are not meant to last forever. If an organization or even a movement fades, it doesn't mean its work was irrelevant. Verta Taylor writes about social movement abeyance, where the most visible forms of movement activity may stop for a period of time only to be taken up later in a new formation. The organizations themselves may disappear, but their work or their influence continues.

But I don't think that the Movement for Black Lives is over. If nothing else, the political impact of their decade or more of work will continue for some time. And their wins shape politics today. Because of their existence then and to some degree now in Chicago, we were able to elect a progressive Black mayor, Brandon Johnson, our former progressive Black state prosecutor, Kim Foxx, and progressive members of DSA to the city council. Their presence meant an expansion in the number of jobs for young people in Chicago, the reinstalling of mental health clinics through the Treatment Not Trauma campaign, and the revoking of cash bail in Illinois. Organizations like BYP100, Dream Defenders, and the coalition of organizations under the Movement for Black Lives provided a political home for young people led by other young people. They built an expansive political education project, sharpening political analysis and discourse in and outside of Black communities. They highlighted Black feminist approaches to strategy, analysis, and leadership. And they helped disseminate and popularize new political frameworks such as abolition. To understand all that these organizations won and their impact on our political landscape, I would recommend Barbara Ransby's *Making All Black Lives Matter: Reimagining Freedom in the Twenty-first Century* or Deva Woodly's *Reckoning: Black Lives Matter and the Democratic Necessity of Social Movements*.

But we should be honest about the fact that many of the movement organizations that emerged after the murder of Trayvon Martin faced real challenges and sometimes failed. I think some became too dependent on philanthropy—and money in general—instead of building a larger volunteer base. Their barriers for entry were sometimes too high and the pathways to engagement for a larger population were sometimes nonexistent.

There's also the question of whether the organizations that we label BLM reached into and built inside Black working-class and poor communities. There's an argument that they did not, but I think the answer is a bit more complicated. I know that there were poor and working-class Black people, young Black people in those organizations and in their leadership, but I don't think the campaigns coming out of those organizations consistently targeted the organizing of Black working-class and poor people and communities. Another difficulty faced by these organizations was the work of what it meant to build and be a political home for folks who are on the margins of society and the margins of Black communities. Sometimes the work of building a political home for folks that protects them from daily attacks on one's body and being may become so consuming that the collective politics of resistance and organizing become less of a priority.

And then there was the challenge of building democratic forms of accountability and participation among a population that's rightly skeptical of organizations, centralized power, and money. These organizations faced enormous challenges. Sometimes they navigated them well and other times they didn't. We have to hold up and celebrate their wins, try to assess their impact by looking at their long-term impact, and also learn from their challenges—and, yes, their failures.

I try to learn from every political experience. So, for example, while BLM rejected the approach of having one charismatic male leader, we still have yet to figure out what a fully accountable and functioning democratic process looks like in movement organizations even if they're "leaderful"—where some people are given the opportunity to become, if not a figurehead for, then a figure publicly associated with the movement. That's not an indictment. Our thinking about what accountability looks like just has to evolve. How do we build in and guarantee greater transparency?

This generation of activist organizers also took seriously self-care and self-preservation, a position I have learned to appreciate. However, at times, I—and others of earlier generations—wondered if the focus on self-care was getting in the way of the work. Many of the young people that I know and love would say, "Oh, you're wrong on this, Cathy." And I totally get the need to preserve people's ability to do the hard work of activism and organizing. But I think it has to be balanced with actually doing the work. I'm not sure that balance was always right at times.

Again, there are many more things that this recent generation of activists have taught me and helped me to rethink—not least of which is how we can not only center poor and working-class people in our campaigns, but build political homes and institutions full of and accountable to those same communities. Of course, as folks are organized into movement spaces, they must feel safe, taken care of, and heard. But, as I mentioned earlier, there is a tension between creating those institutions and moving beyond those institutions to do the work of movement building. We have to be building political homes while also doing the door-knocking and organizing that builds power and changes lives. The duality of that work can be hard to hold. It is something I probably didn't think enough about.



**BT:** And it speaks to that tension self-care creates—between the feeling of being at home and those difficult outward-facing demands for a more inclusive movement.

**CC:** Exactly. Then we also have to be prepared to deal with harm—and to navigate, which I think most of these organizations did, instances of harm inflicted too often by men on women. How do we deal with harm while also committing to not discarding anyone? What does it mean to take harm seriously, but also to take the learning, evolution, and care of those who've caused harm seriously? We're asking a lot of these organizations relating to violence and care. Sometimes they handle such challenges well, and sometimes they don't, but their effort to engage this challenge will inform how people move forward and build movements in the future.

**BT:** Your classic essay, "Punks, Bulldaggers, and Welfare Queens: The Radical Potential of Queer Politics?" helped a generation of readers articulate deep frustrations with the political rhetoric and strategies in civil rights activism, and offered a kind of queer politics as a radical alternative. People keep returning to it in part because you draw a sharp distinction between "civil rights-based" inclusion and a radical queer politics committed to unsettling the hierarchies and identity categories that structure domination. You also critique the presumed opposition between "mainstream" and "queer," showing how that binary can obscure the messy and contradictory power relations within marginalized queer communities themselves.

**"The right's war on the academy and education is part of a generational war over what young people, especially young white people, will be taught and how they will be socialized."**



Today, criticisms that seem like they target your position on this have gained renewed visibility and support. Andrew Sullivan recently argued in the *New York Times* that the post-*Obergefell* LGBTQ movement overreached—that it should return to a vision of civil rights inclusion and abandon what he calls "radical gender revolution," because the latter is alienating the broader public and threatens to undermine the gains of earlier gay and lesbian activism. He says the movement is intolerant of dissent, obsessed with identity proliferation, and dangerously focused on youth and educational institutions. Congresswoman Sarah McBride has a similar view: she argues that some trans activists overplayed their hand and abandoned the politics of persuasion, losing the support of sympathetic liberals in the process. How do you respond to these accounts? Do they get anything right, or is this simply the latest chapter in the recurring debate between integration and transformation?

**CC:** Sullivan has always promoted a liberal, reductive understanding of LGBTQ politics that seems nostalgic for a time when white gay men were understood as the normative category of gay politics. I'm less persuaded by his call for the simpler times uncomplicated by the different gender, race, and class positions of those he understands to be gay or queer. For me this was a position too often articulated, for example, by some white gay men in the '80s and '90s in ACT UP New York meetings, which I attended and participated in. Those individuals seemed to think that their access to white privilege would be tainted by the non-normative and uncompromising positions of radical queer people who sought freedom, not acceptance from the respectable middle class of gays. The truth is, a politics of inclusion based on the civil rights framework was never meant to address the issues of queers of color and poor and working-class queers, whether they were folks of color or white. Sullivan is interested in a politics of inclusion where we conform to hetero- and homo-normative standards and, as a reward, are included—allowed to marry and serve in the military, and accepted because we demand little or nothing from the state.



I count myself among those who believe that same-sex marriage only helps to legitimize a process intent on producing a hierarchy of citizenship and rights bolstered by the institution of marriage. In the 2000s, gay leadership largely sought normality: marriage, military, and electoral power. The cost, of course, of being on the other side of normal, as Michael Warner, Lauren Berlant, Lisa Duggan, and others have warned, is that you must participate in the process of excluding those deemed "deviants" and give up on the cause of radical transformation. It produces, as Duggan explains, a depoliticized, privatized gay community committed to shrinking gay public spaces while expanding the gay market and consumption. So for me, that makes Sullivan's critique problematic and really not new.

Now, McBride's argument is different. There is something to her demand that we engage people continuously, moving them to our position and being informed by people's concerns, even their apprehension—and yes, their misinformation too. I try to say this repeatedly about all sectors of politics, not only queer politics: we have to persuade, we have to organize, we have to talk to people, we have to engage with folks and their ideas to move them to our side and to have our side informed by people's lives. We have to be committed to building sustainable power. To do so, we need to think about how we can build a majority around our positions. How are we organizing people to our positions? How are we winning their hearts and minds? If we are truly trying to expand our base so that we can move a left agenda meant to radically transform people's lives, we have to take McBride's argument a bit more seriously than I take Sullivan's position.

**BT:** *Boundaries of Blackness* is a book that changed my life. It helped me understand a lot more about the community I grew up in—in particular, the way people treated queer people in my family and the things they were trying to work through, often in spaces that weren't visible to everyone else. That affected what I thought were some of the central questions of Black politics. So when people ask me, "What should I read?" I often recommend your book. Let me ask you the same: What have you read that has fundamentally shaped you as a thinker, and is there something you wish more people were reading now?

**CC:** There are so many texts that have influenced my thinking, but I'll give you three. As a budding Black feminist, bell hooks's *Feminist Theory: From Margin to Center* was a critical text. It taught me the limits of second-wave feminist theory and what happens when we allow ourselves to center the people around us. For me that was the experiences of Black women. How does that change not only the stories we tell, but the theories we produce and the political work we pursue?

Another was James C. Scott's *Domination and the Arts of Resistance*. It reminded me to be attuned to the ways that people are consistently, and sometimes in cloaked ways, engaged in resisting their oppression. In political science, there is a standard way that we operationalize something we might call "politics," but Scott suggested that people are always thinking, collaborating, and evolving in the ways they preserve limited agency. That emphasis on quotidian power was an important lesson.

The third book is Manning Marable's *Race, Reform and Rebellion: The Second Reconstruction in Black America, 1945–1982*. Manning himself had a huge impression on me. He was a generous scholar and mentor, and he modeled what it meant to be *in* the academy but not *of* the academy. He took data and statistics seriously as another method of conveying the complexity and beauty of Black people. And his book was important for me in its thinking through of the multiple dimensions of resistance in the history of Black people.

All these texts have changed how I think about my work—and especially in the ways that work can move outside the academy and have an impact on the work of activists and organizers.

**BT:** You have moved creatively between different communities: mentoring youth activists, participating in local government, teaching in local high schools, helping organize academics for political change. What have you learned in practice about the relationship between academic work and political organizing?

**CC:** My work outside of the academy has everything to do with my discomfort within it. I come from a working-class family in Toledo, Ohio, that has experienced both the opportunities provided by the welfare state and the penalties extracted from the carceral state. I was a first-generation college student, and I remember feeling like I never fully understood what was expected of me in college and grad school. It wasn't that I didn't understand the work and assignments in those environments—it was the culture of the institutions, even among the Black people there. Since I never felt fully at home, I was always committed to expanding, and hopefully transforming, the academy so people like me could be there and I would feel less like an outsider.

I also come from a family where union organizing and political engagement—whether through electoral politics, movements, or the church—was expected. I bring that instinct with me into the academy. The people I gravitated to, especially at the University of Michigan, where I was in graduate school, were the scholar-activists. I became friends and chosen family with folks like Barbara Ransby, Tracye Matthews, Premilla Nadasen, Kim Smith, Jocelyn Sargent, and Regina Freer. I was taught by folks like Robin D. G. Kelley, Michael Dawson, Tom Holt, and Elsa Barkley Brown. Thus, I was welcomed into a community who understood its work to be both learning and making legible the complicated and beautiful histories, politics, and intimacies of often-ignored communities, especially Black communities, but also transforming institutions of higher education.

At this very dangerous moment, some will turn to the scholar-activist model. That is fine. But I might suggest a more intentional focus on how we think about and build a broad movement in the academy—one intent on reimagining the university and our role in it. I am grateful to be working with an amazing group of comrades in the organization Scholars for Social Justice (SSJ), a group that believes we must work with an expansive analysis of the academy and the work of universities. As Davarian Baldwin, another member of SSJ, highlights in his wonderful book *In the Shadow of the Ivory Tower: How Universities Are Plundering Our Cities,* we have to understand that the university extends beyond what we do in the classroom to include running police forces and charter schools and being an employer, health care provider, and landlord.

Folks in SSJ also recognize that the dismantling of the academy through an attack on critical race theory and DEI was never enough for this administration, so it has also mobilized claims of rampant antisemitism and threats to safety to justify the imposition of policies meant to end student protest in general and especially protests against the genocide and humanitarian crisis in Gaza. Therefore, we must organize on our campuses and across our campuses to build power. That means we have to talk to colleagues we normally would not. We have to do one-on-ones with folks in and out of the university about the issues that are important to them. We might start with the topic of faculty governance or the deporting of students in their labs and move on from there.





**BT:** I think many faculty want to start with the defense of academic freedom. What do you think universities and faculty members ought to do to today preserve our precarious scholarly freedom — especially those of us interested in questions of class conflict, ethnic and religious violence, or hierarchies built on race, gender, and sexuality?

**CC:** Truthfully, while academic freedom is something we should defend, especially as it provides a platform for allowing faculty to teach and say what they want, I don't believe that is the primary struggle that should animate our work right now. As I argued earlier, we have to understand that the right sees its war on the academy and education in general as part of a generational war over what young people, especially young white people, will be taught, how they will be socialized, and how they will align themselves politically. We have to also understand this as a battle for the power to shape the political terrain on which we will define truth, facts, and history.

As Trump seeks to shrink the higher education sector, we have to make a claim for providing more access to folks who want a college education. And as Trump asks students and families to take on more debt to go to college, we have to demand that more colleges are free for the public. As Trump seeks to control administrators, we have to demand that faculty, students, staff, and community members have more power throughout higher education, including on schools' boards of trustees. Only with the most expansive conceptualization of the university and the centralized financial and political power of the board of trustees can we effectively mount resistance and reimagine the work of the academy during these very dangerous times. **BR**

# GAZA AND THE END OF HISTORY

*Joelle M. Abi-Rached*

Image: AP

**DURING A RECENT PANEL** on Gaza and human rights held in Bangkok, I was asked whether the destruction of Gaza represents a watershed moment for the twenty-first century. The answer, of course, is unequivocally in the affirmative. Nearly two years into Israel's onslaught, we have heard something like this claim made many times: there is the world before this annihilation, and the world after. Have we really understood what this means?

Gaza's utterly ruined landscape serves as a mirror, reflecting the ultimate *reductio ad absurdum* of the liberal international order. Israel's unchecked bombardment not just of Gaza but of Lebanon, Iran, Yemen, and now Syria; its unprecedented and systematic devastation of health care systems and the most basic infrastructure for sustaining human life; its blockade of humanitarian aid, attacks at food distribution sites, and use of starvation as an instrument of collective punishment; its criminal disregard for the murders and land grabs committed by settlers in the West Bank—the totality of this relentless aggression, captured only in part by this morbid catalogue and compounded by every mechanism of rationalization and denial, reveals the complete erosion of international humanitarian law, the double standards that govern the rhetoric of human rights, and the racism that sits at the core of the West's strained efforts to maintain geopolitical hegemony. A poll conducted by researchers at Pennsylvania State University and reported in *Haaretz* earlier this year found that 82 percent of Israeli Jews support expelling Palestinians from Gaza, 56 percent support expelling Israel's own Arab citizens, 47 percent endorse the Israel Defense Forces acting "as Joshua did in Jericho—kill all its inhabitants," and, among those who see Palestinians as Amalek, 93 percent believe the biblical injunction to "wipe out Amalek" still applies. As of this writing in late July, the magnitude of the hunger crisis is eliciting the strongest criticism of Israeli actions in Western media seen since the siege began, while two prominent Israeli humanitarian organizations, Physicians for Human Rights and B'Tselem, have joined the judgment of multiple other scholars and groups around the globe in declaring that Israel is committing genocide. What becomes of democracy, human rights, and moral responsibility in the face of all this?



Pankaj Mishra provides an answer in his recent book, *The World After Gaza*, which situates Israel's genocidal campaign within a larger continuum of Western imperialism, entrenched racism, and colonial legacies. Among its many effects, what is being done to the people of Gaza—and what the United States continues to enable—is forcing a global reckoning as the West's self-portrait as guardian of universal values decisively cracks under the weight of its complicity. Though long in the making, the unraveling is now more acute than at any time since the end of the Cold War.

**Gaza has become a symbol both of Western hypocrisy and of its victims' recourse to human rights and international law as a final forum for collective deliverance.**

The evidence is on wide display and only mounting. In a July speech at an emergency meeting of the Hague Group, a global alliance convened by the Progressive International in January to hold Israel accountable under international law, Colombian President Gustavo Petro offered a frankly dystopian interpretation to the thirty-two nations in attendance in Bogotá. "Gaza," he said, "is simply an experiment by the ultra-rich, trying to show all the people of the world how to respond to humanity's rebellion." "They plan to bomb all of us," he added, then clarified—"those of us in the Global South, at least." Invoking the bombing of Guernica during the Spanish Civil War, he stressed that another of the casualties of this "barbarism" is multilateralism itself—the "chance for nations to come together," the very "idea of global democracy" and its international institutions.

Of course, as Sven Lindqvist recounts in *A History of Bombing* (2000), colonial powers routinely bombed defenseless civilian populations, from Italian campaigns in Libya to British attacks in India and all over the Middle East; it was the European setting of Guernica that imbued its destruction with moral urgency for the West and gave its crimes a historical salience the victims of colonialism had always been denied. Today, growing solidarity with Gaza is perceived by so many in the West as a threat to Western interests and values precisely because it purports to extend moral concern to the "wrong" victims. It is no coincidence that seventeen of the twenty countries that have joined South Africa's case charging Israel with genocide at the International Court of Justice are from the so-called Global South.





Gaza has thus become a symbol both of Western hypocrisy and of its victims' recourse to human rights and international law as a final forum of appeal for collective deliverance—the deliverance of the "wretched of the earth," as Frantz Fanon famously called colonized subjects, whoever and wherever they may be. The legal and moral reverberations cannot be overstated, for the global order and for the future of humanity.

---

**AMONG THE TRAGEDIES** of the ongoing destruction is the apparent repetition of an ancient pattern, an eternal return of history from which Gaza cannot seem to escape. One of the oldest continuously inhabited cities on earth, it has been repeatedly destroyed and rebuilt over centuries. *Venit calvitium super Gazam*, "Baldness has come upon Gaza," reads the opening of Jeremiah 47:5 in the Vulgate. In *Jewish Antiquities*, Flavius Josephus tells how Gaza was attacked in the mid-second century BCE by Jonathan Maccabeus, who during the struggles between Demetrius II and Antiochus VI reached Gaza only to be shut out; in revenge he besieged it, plundered its suburbs, then accepted a plea for peace and took hostages to Jerusalem.

Decades later, after a protracted siege ending around 96 BCE, the Judean King Alexander Jannaeus captured Gaza, totally devastating it as part of his coastal expansion. The city lay desolate until it was restored to independence by the Roman general and statesman Pompey and rebuilt on or near a new site by the proconsul Aulus Gabinius in 57 BCE. It prospered again under early Roman rule, and then, with the first Jewish–Roman revolt in 66 CE, Judean extremists destroyed it once again. "Neither Sebaste nor Ashkelon withstood their fury," Josephus writes. "These they burnt to the ground and then razed Anthedon and Gaza. In the vicinity of each of these cities many villages were pillaged and immense numbers of the inhabitants captured and slaughtered."

The Jews were not the only ones to hate the "Gazaians," as Josephus called the region's inhabitants. In 395 AD, Porphyrius was appointed bishop of Gaza and set about converting the city's predominantly pagan population, often through coercive measures that included the demolition of their temples and the repurposing of sacred spaces for Christian worship. Today, the bishop is considered one of the early saints of the Eastern Orthodox and Catholic traditions. In 1150, a church bearing his name was erected on the foundations of a fifth-century church dedicated to him—the very church that was shelled by the Israeli army on October 20, 2023, killing eighteen people as hundreds of Christians and Muslims were taking shelter there. A central moment in the *Life of Saint Porphyrius*, written by the bishop's deacon Mark, is the destruction of the Temple of Marnas, presented as a triumph over idolatry. Mark records how the people of Gaza were forced to watch their most important religious sanctuary being destroyed by imperial troops, instigated by the bishop and a mob of vengeful Christians.

The French historian Jean-Pierre Filiu chronicles this *longue durée* in *Gaza: A History* (2014), tracing the siege of this tiny strip of land down to the contemporary world—through the Nakba, Israeli occupation after 1967, and the establishment of a total blockade upon the withdrawal of Israeli settlers in 2005—while capturing the real scale of historical time, political agency, and global significance of the region. The fact that even the broad sweep of this history remains virtually unknown, despite the prominence of Israel-Palestine in the foreign policy of Western governments for decades, is itself a measure of the depth of dehumanization to which Palestinians have always been subject in public consciousness in the West—reduced, at best, to alien Others or blank victims without a culture and without a past, and usually portrayed as much worse. "So much of our history has been occluded," Edward Said noted in 1999. "We are invisible people." The same remains true more than a quarter-century later.

Western powers' reactions to the litany of Israeli military operations in Gaza in the recent past—Cast Lead in 2008–9, Pillar of Defense in 2012, Protective Edge in 2014, the air strikes of 2021—themselves followed a recurring trend: initial affirmation of Israel's "right to self-defense" and "right to exist," followed at most by muted or delayed criticism of disproportionate force once it is a *fait accompli*, and always minimal political or diplomatic consequences, if any at all. All the while, Israel imposed conditions on Gaza that culminated in growing global outrage at confining its two million residents to an "open-air prison."



Well before the current genocide, then, countless scholars and human rights organizations were condemning an obvious double standard: while professing commitments to human rights and international law, Western governments fueled their subversion by failing to hold Israel accountable and directly aiding its crimes. The pattern of exoneration—the rigorously enforced indifference to the "victims of the victims"—warrants a psychoanalytic inquiry unto itself. Implicating unresolved guilt over the Shoah, compounded by an inability to regard Arabic-speaking peoples and Muslims as fully human, it reflects an insidious modern form of antisemitism, which on the one hand insists on support for Israel as the *sine qua non* of Jewishness and on the other collapses prejudice against a people into contestation of contingent state actions.

But the destruction this time, however continuous with a long history of oppression, is different. In addition to the apocalyptic scale of death and devastation, unseen in the previous fourteen wars on Gaza since the Nakba, there is, first, the reckoning that Mishra tracks: the death knell for whatever moral authority the West struggled to retain and project since the U.S. invasion of Iraq, the Bush administration's use of torture (for which it has never faced accountability), and its declaration of a "global war on terror" after September 11. By underwriting Israel's genocidal onslaught—financially, materially, and ideologically—so flagrantly these twenty-two months and counting, Western governments have hastened the final discrediting of the rules-based legal order that the West itself developed in the wreckage of World War II, structured around the four interlocking norms of the illegality of aggressive war, universal human rights and civilian protection, accountability for atrocity crimes, and multilateral cooperation.

The cases of Ireland, Spain, and Norway, which recognized the state of Palestine in May last year, are the exceptions that prove the rule. After the International Criminal Court (ICC) issued an arrest warrant for Israeli Prime Minister Benjamin Netanyahu in November, leaders in Germany, Italy, and Poland vowed not to arrest Netanyahu or extradite him to the Hague should he visit their countries. For its part, the United States has imposed sanctions on Karim Khan, the ICC's chief prosecutor, and Francesca Albanese, the UN's Special Rapporteur on human rights in the Palestinian territories, while Netanyahu has entered the country three times since February. Emmanuel Macron's late-breaking declaration that France will recognize Palestinian statehood at the United Nations this September follows his initial strong support for Israel for months after October 7 and the country's argument that the ICC warrant is invalid because Israel is not a member of the court.

**By underwriting Israel's genocidal onslaught so flagrantly, Western powers have hastened the discrediting of the liberal international order the West itself developed after World War II.**

In so decisively shredding the norms they helped establish, together with their associated moral and legal architecture—the UN Declaration of Human Rights of 1948, the Geneva Conventions of 1949, the Nuremberg Principles of 1950, the Rome Statute of 1998—Western powers are presiding over the final collapse of their credibility in ways they do not appear to recognize or understand. The morbid systems are manifesting in the wider world, however. At recent conferences I attended in Cairo, Beirut, and Bangkok, variously focused on the future of capitalism, the long-term sequelae of historical trauma, and the fate of human rights discourse, young students and junior scholars from the Global South argued for a decisive turn away from intellectual, political, and moral frameworks associated with the West.

The impulse is understandable, and the critique should not be taken lightly. But there are profound costs to renouncing the universalism of human rights as nothing but a sham, intrinsically compromised by its affiliation with Western hypocrisy or its corruption by Western power.

Doing so risks entrenching a West-East/North-South divide and fueling an "us versus them" dynamic reminiscent of Samuel P. Huntington's "clash of civilizations." It also sets a perilous precedent for future violence, aggression, and war unchecked by even imperfect appeals to shared norms and values. In this regard, leading humanitarian organizations and think tanks—including Oxfam, the Overseas Development Institute, and the UN World Food Programme—have warned that Israel's obstruction of relief efforts in Gaza threatens to undermine humanitarian responses in the roughly 130 other armed or protracted conflicts worldwide. As the president of the International Committee of the Red Cross, Mirjana Spoljaric Egger, further reminded the UN Security Council Open Debate on the Protection of Civilians in Armed Conflict in May, ignoring these rules is "a race to the moral bottom—a fast track to chaos and irreversible despair."



For countless people around the world, particularly where democratic and liberal aspirations are relentlessly attacked and appeals to human rights remain the primary defense against authoritarian rule, the erosion of the credibility of the fundamental norms of the postwar order profoundly undermines ongoing political struggles against injustice. In his important book published earlier this year, *Righting Wrongs*, Kenneth Roth, the long-time director of Human Rights Watch, persuasively argues that exposing atrocities and advocating for justice is not merely a moral imperative but a crucial, oftentimes the only, means of holding power accountable on the global stage. International law and the broader human rights architecture are more than just a framework for an internal order that strives for peace and justice; they constitute a lifeline toward a fairer, more equitable future. Handing autocrats, tyrants, and oligarchs a regime of purely transactional governance with no accountability mechanism—where human rights cease to be intrinsic and legally enshrined and instead become arbitrary—would be our gravest mistake. Petro thus spoke in Bogotá of the need both to condemn prevailing "barbarism" and to give real meaning to the principles now being betrayed—to keep alive, that is, "the possibility of another kind of humanity, one that can love and think collectively." As his work with the Hague Group makes clear, it has fallen to the Global South to carry that torch and lead the struggle for genuine equality and justice following the eclipse of Western integrity. Our best course is to keep pressing for critical engagement, exposing and challenging the West's blind spots, double standards, racism, and imperial abuses while simultaneously advancing the universal human-rights framework.

A second aspect of the ongoing onslaught that stands out relative to the past is the unprecedented weaponization and systematic destruction of the right to health and health care—that is, the right to life itself. The horrific figures are by now well-known: the thousands of children killed, the thousands with limbs amputated, the irreversible damage to surviving bodies and minds. While health and health care have been attacked in previous conflicts and continue to be attacked in Ukraine, Sudan, and other conflicts around the world, never before has an entire health care system been systematically pulverized as a military strategy, nor have we seen so many health care professionals being systematically targeted, kidnapped, abused, and tortured. According to a World Health Organization database, more than two-thirds of all global attacks on health care were perpetrated in Gaza and the West Bank since October 7.

In a remarkable editorial published in May this year, *The Lancet*, one of the most impactful medical journals in the world, finally deplored the "silence and impunity" on Gaza. The editorial contends that Gaza's health catastrophe—which public health experts around the world have warned about incessantly and to no avail—is no longer just a crisis of military violence but a crisis of global complicity: silence from health institutions and paralysis at the UN Security Council are enabling these ongoing blatant violations of international humanitarian law. Ending that silence, the editorial insists, is a professional and moral duty for the global health community and a prerequisite for protecting civilian lives.

Over thirty-two days last winter, Filiu himself documented conditions in Gaza while embedded with a Médecins Sans Frontières team stationed in the so-called "humanitarian zone" in central and southern Gaza. The only professional Western historian to my knowledge to have seen the devastation firsthand, his eyewitness testimony melds visceral reportage—nighttime convoys through a landscape of endless rubble, stories of families repeatedly displaced, hospitals deliberately hit—with a historian's long view of Gaza's entrapment since 1967. Extracts of his diary, published by *Le Monde* earlier this year, echo the reports of

Palestinians, doctors, and humanitarian groups over the last two years, portraying a territory subjected to what he describes as a methodical project of expulsion and destruction—in other words, the very definition of ethnic cleansing. His purpose, Filiu explains, was to contribute further direct evidence of the atrocities being committed that would otherwise remain unseen while Israel blocks international media access and to combat the "historical revisionism" of "Western governments, intellectual elites, and mainstream media," despite the constant stream of videos, images, pleas, and reports that have flooded out of Gaza from the beginning. It is another stark measure of the dehumanization and racism at the core of the West's alliance with Israel that these direct Palestinian testimonies have scarcely been heard or heeded in Western media, generally dismissed as antisemitic lies or Hamas propaganda while the claims of the Israeli army and government are reported and reflexively trusted without the most basic scrutiny.

**In July, Colombian President Gustavo Petro spoke of the need both to condemn the "barbarism" and to keep alive "the possibility of another kind of humanity, one that can love and think collectively."**

And now, Gaza is starving, prompting a far too belated outpouring of alarm from Western elites. UNICEF has said that more than 9,000 children have been treated for malnutrition in Gaza this year. According to a May report from the World Health Organization, "This is one of the world's worst hunger crises, unfolding in real time," with "the entire 2.1 million population of Gaza . . . facing prolonged food shortages, with nearly half a million people in a catastrophic situation of hunger, acute malnutrition, starvation, illness and death." In the wake of this news, seven European countries said in a joint statement that they "will not be silent in front of the man-made humanitarian catastrophe that is taking place before our eyes in Gaza," and the EU started a review of its trade agreement with Israel.The situation has only declined since then, reaching such a paroxysm of catastrophe that outrage has begun to reach across partisan divides and into the pages of the *New York Times*.

Why now? Why, after twenty-two months of complacency and complicity, have some European and American elites suddenly changed their tone? The conceit that the basic facts or circumstances have changed—that real alarm was inappropriate until now—defies all serious analysis. Is it rather because starvation has long been the Achilles' heel of imperial adventurism, a moral bridge too far for the enlightened nations? It would be flattering to the West to think so, but the shift instead looks driven by utilitarian considerations: an attempt to salvage some credibility in the face of plummeting popular support, and perhaps the belated recognition that, left completely unchecked, Netanyahu's expansionist ambitions—to annex the West Bank and Gaza Strip—spell disaster for the West's own interests.

---

**GAZA, THEN,** is much more than a "humanitarian catastrophe." It is a turning point that lays bare the full range and cruel depths of the contemporary world's contradictions—the unreconstructed moral biases and prejudices of entire populations, the fractures within nominally democratic polities, and the apparent fragility, even occasional futility, of resistance. It shows how swiftly majorities can capitulate, whether for survival or out of self-interest, and it exposes what is fundamentally wrong today: a persistent inability to recognize every human being as equal and deserving of dignity and life, whatever their beliefs, skin color, or religious affiliation. The universal human-rights framework has been totally eviscerated and lies in urgent need of repair. The United Nations itself—indispensable yet increasingly impotent—needs a fundamental reset. We cannot afford to revert to the pre–human rights era while regimes slide into authoritarianism, bigotry is rampant, xenophobia endures, and liberal democracy remains, for many, only an aspiration.

Filiu's documentary testimony evokes the work of Simone Weil, the formidable philosopher-activist who traveled to Germany in 1932 to observe the rise of Hitler firsthand. While many of her contemporaries watched from afar—oblivious to Germany's rapid descent into Nazism and the early persecution of Jews that followed Hitler's appointment as chancellor in January 1933—Weil produced one of the earliest, clearest autopsies of the Weimar Republic's collapse. Her prescient observations teach us that nations require "roots" in compassion and that only unconditional obligations to every person can keep the modern world from relapsing into perpetual war.

The so-called "advanced liberal democracies" of the West were identified so strongly with these principles during the second half of the twentieth century that with the collapse of the Soviet Union, Francis Fukuyama could argue, to a chorus of agreement, that liberal democracy had triumphed as the terminus of history's ideological development. The ongoing genocide in Gaza reveals that the contest over political legitimacy, human rights, and state sovereignty was always far from settled—that history's conflicts over power, identity, and justice will persist until the claims of humanity reach "the last man." **BR**

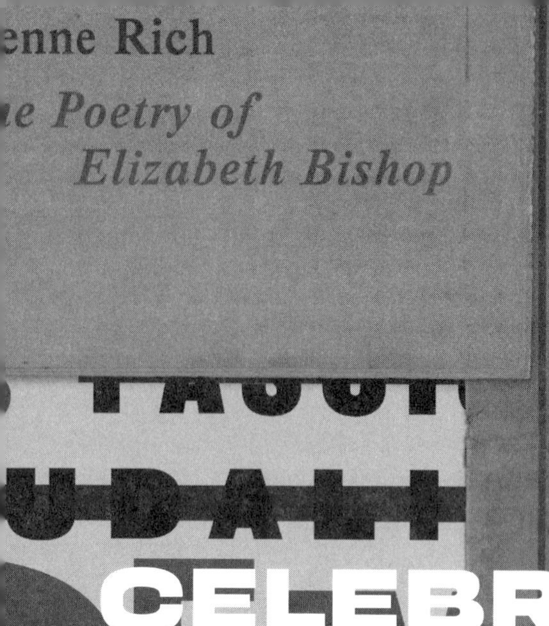
enne Rich
e Poetry of
Elizabeth Bishop

*BOSTON REVIEW* **HAS TURNED FIFTY.** To celebrate this milestone, fifty writers and editors selected notable pieces from our archive and shared what they admire about them. Describing work that ranges from war reporting to cultural criticism to philosophical argument, "rigorous" and "startling" essays to debate-defining writing about our political, economic, and social arrangements, they praise *Boston Review* pieces for their "remarkable prescience" and "reasoned compassion," for being "revelatory" and "essential" and "alive to the world." We are grateful for their words—and proud, as one writer puts it, to have developed a reputation as "a vital venue for discussions of how to build a more just world."

What follows is a selection of these appreciations, together with a short excerpt from the original essay. To read them all, visit bostonreview.net/celebrating-50-years.

# NOAM CHOMSKY'S ESSAYS

Despite being one of the world's most cited intellectuals, Noam Chomsky has often been excluded from mainstream political discourse. Even though many of his observations about the criminal destructiveness of U.S. wars have been vindicated over time, his sharp critiques of American foreign policy were consigned to those few publications that take seriously the obligation to hear a wide range of points of view. *Boston Review* has been one of those publications, over the years publishing powerful essays like Chomsky's review of Stanley Karnow's popular Vietnam War history (1984), his essay on whether states ever undertake "humanitarian interventions" (1993), his analysis of the Bush administration's "grand strategy" (2003), and his revisiting of his classic 1967 essay "The Responsibility of Intellectuals" on the tenth anniversary of September 11, excerpted here. These are important pieces that shine a light on some of the most uncomfortable truths about our country. And as Chomsky himself has recognized, it's hard to think of a magazine other than *Boston Review* that would have published them.

**—Nathan J. Robinson, editor of *Current Affairs***

**THE PATTERN** of praise and punishment is a familiar one throughout history: those who line up in the service of the state are typically praised by the general intellectual community, and those who refuse to line up in service of the state are punished. Thus in retrospect Woodrow Wilson and the progressive intellectuals who offered him their services are greatly honored, but not Eugene Debs. Rosa Luxemburg and Karl Liebknecht were murdered and have hardly been heroes of the intellectual mainstream. Bertrand Russell continued to be bitterly condemned until after his death—and in current biographies still is. . . .

It seems to be close to a historical universal that conformist intellectuals, the ones who support official aims and ignore or rationalize official crimes, are honored and privileged in their own societies, and the value-oriented punished in one or another way. The pattern goes back to the earliest records. It was the man accused of corrupting the youth of Athens who drank the hemlock, much as Dreyfusards were accused of "corrupting souls, and, in due course, society as a whole" and the value-oriented intellectuals of the 1960s were charged with interference with "indoctrination of the young."

In the Hebrew scriptures there are figures who by contemporary standards are dissident intellectuals, called "prophets" in the English translation. They bitterly angered the establishment with their critical geopolitical analysis, their condemnation of the crimes of the powerful, their calls for justice and concern for the poor and suffering. King Ahab, the most evil of the kings, denounced the Prophet Elijah as a hater of Israel, the first "self-hating Jew" or "anti-American" in the modern counterparts. The prophets were treated harshly, unlike the flatterers at the court, who were later condemned as false prophets. The pattern is understandable. It would be surprising if it were otherwise.

As for the responsibility of intellectuals, there does not seem to me to be much to say beyond some simple truths. Intellectuals are typically privileged—merely an observation about usage of the term. Privilege yields opportunity, and opportunity confers responsibilities. An individual then has choices.

# ELAINE SCARRY
## CITIZENSHIP IN EMERGENCY



In *Thought Reform and the Psychology of Totalism: A Study of "Brainwashing" in China*, Robert Jay Lifton coined the phrase "thought-terminating cliché" to describe how leaders of coercive institutions delimit subjects' very ability to imagine any reality beyond that defined by the cult. Nations suffer under thought-terminating clichés, too—America, no more so than when it comes to the concepts subsumed under the umbrella "national security," which is how we manage to imagine how a military bigger than the next nine biggest combined could protect, defend, and preserve a constitutional order that originally considered standing armies anathema to the security of a free nation. I'll never forget how it felt to read Elaine Scarry blowing those clichés wide open with "Citizenship in Emergency," comparing how the entire elephantine American military bureaucracy failed to protect the nation on September 11, 2001, to the way the citizens aboard Flight 93 succeeded in protecting it—by acting precisely like the sort of self-organized citizen militia the Founders imagined. Provocations to thinking in place of thought-terminating clichés: that is what *Boston Review* does so well.

**—Rick Perlstein, contributing editor at *In These Times***

**WHEN THE PLANE** that hit the Pentagon and the plane that crashed in Pennsylvania are looked at side by side, they reveal two different conceptions of national defense: one model is authoritarian, centralized, top down; the other, operating in a civil frame, is distributed and egalitarian. Should anything be inferred from the fact that the first form of defense failed and the second succeeded? This outcome obligates us to review our military structures, and to consider the possibility that we need a democratic, not a top-down, form of defense. At the very least, the events of September 11 cast doubt on a key argument that, for the past fifty years, has been used to legitimize an increasingly centralized, authoritarian model of defense—namely the argument from speed. . . .

We have witnessed many actions taken in the name of homeland defense that are independent of, or external to, civilian control. Foreign residents have been seized and placed in circumstances that violate our most basic laws; the war against Afghanistan was underway before we had even been given much explanation of its connection to the terrorists, who were all from Saudi Arabia or Lebanon or Egypt or the United Arab Emirates and not from Afghanistan; that war now seems to be over even though we don't know whether we eliminated the small circle around Osama bin Laden, for whose sake we believed we were there; we are now tripping rapidly ahead to the next war, listening passively to weekly announcements about an approaching war with Iraq that has no visible connection to the events of September 11; the president's formulation of this future war sometimes seems to include (or at least not to exclude) the use of nuclear weapons and the animation of our nuclear first-use policy. The decoupling of all defense from the population itself lurches between large outcomes (presidential declaration of war) and the texture of everyday life. . . .

We are defending the country by ceding our own powers of self-defense to a set of managers external to ourselves. But can these powers be ceded without relinquishing the very destination toward which we were traveling together, as surely as if our ship had been seized? The destination for which we purchased tickets was a country where no one was arrested without their names being made public, a country that did not carry out wars without the authorization of Congress, a country that does not threaten to use weapons of mass destruction. Why are we sitting quietly in our seats?

# JOSEPH H. CARENS
# THE CASE FOR AMNESTY

Over the years, I have kept returning to Joseph Carens's forum essay, "The Case for Amnesty," and the responses to it. Carens's argument—that irregular migrants who have established long-term ties in a country deserve legal status—emphasizes the role of time in developing social links with host communities and rules out harsh measures such as deportation. It is as philosophically compelling as it is politically urgent, the more polarized and ideologically driven discussions surrounding migration become. Both the article and the responses exemplify what *Boston Review* does best, fostering debate that connects theory with real-world political challenges, speaking across divides, showing us that one does not need to sacrifice philosophical rigor to deliver sound policy advice.

**—Lea Ypi, political theorist and author of *Free***

**MOST PEOPLE THINK** that the state has the right to determine whom it will admit and to apprehend and deport migrants who settle without official authorization. Let us accept that conventional view about states and borders as a premise and explore the question of whether a state nonetheless may sometimes be morally obliged to grant legal-resident status to irregular migrants. . . .

How can migrants become members of society without legal authorization? Because social membership does not depend upon official permission: this is the crux of my argument. People who live and work and raise their families in a society become members, whatever their legal status: that is why we find it hard to expel them when they are discovered. Their presence may be against the law, but that does not make them criminals. It would be wrong to force them to leave once they have become members, even when we have reasons for wanting them to go and for preventing others like them from coming.

Over time the circumstances of entry grow less important. Eventually, they become altogether irrelevant. . . . Settling without authorization violates immigration laws, but that does not mean that we should punish people many years after the fact. As the historian Mae Ngai has argued, there is a parallel between statutes of limitations for criminal offenses and a policy of not deporting long-settled irregular migrants. Most states recognize that the passage of time matters morally, at least for less-serious criminal violations. If a person has not been arrested and charged within a specified period (often three to five years), legal authorities may no longer pursue her for that offense.

Why do states establish statutes of limitations? Because it is not right to make people live indefinitely with a threat of serious legal consequences hanging over their heads for some long-past action, except for the most serious sorts of offenses. Keeping the threat in place for a long period serves no useful deterrent function and causes great harm to the individual—more than is warranted by the original offense. If we are prepared to let time erode the state's power to pursue actual crimes, it makes even more sense to let time erode the power of the state to pursue immigration violations, which are not normally treated as crimes and should not be viewed as crimes.

2016

# VIVIAN GORNICK
## FEELING PARANOID



On the day after Donald Trump's 2016 election, which a lot of us spent doomscrolling, Vivian Gornick sought solace in a 448-page tome on democracy and paranoia in ancient Athens. Her bibliographic reflex brought her to the reasoned compassion that is so characteristic of *Boston Review.* Gornick took the scholarly book's thesis—that societies and individuals thrive or implode depending on whether their paranoias darken into pathology or are defused by a desire to understand "the other"—and illuminated the electoral catastrophe by applying it, brilliantly, to herself. She showed us how the most personal of politicized decisions, her abortion decades earlier, led her to empathize with the very people who would deny her that option. "Feeling Paranoid" demands rereading in the post-*Dobbs* era and our current political season, where the bonfire of conspiratorial rage may yet still be quelled by the empathetic impulse to—as Gornick puts it so well—"honor the existence of the one not like ourselves."

**—Susan Faludi, Pulitzer Prize–winning author of *Backlash***

**FOR PHYLLIS SCHLAFLY,** feminism was the Antichrist, and she would rather have seen America come apart at the seams than submit to our godless demands. . . . She wanted *Roe v. Wade* overturned. She said there was no such thing as rape in marriage and that labor-saving devices such as indoor clothes dryers had provided all the necessary improvements in life that a woman needed.

What was sobering—and what sent us reeling—was the incredible response she received from a few million ordinary women who now seemed to be living in terror of any sort of social change. An old-time revivalist movement seemed to sweep through the land, the kind that arises when a society, like an individual, being forced to face its own deepest conflicts, cries out against the potential loss of familiar dysfunction, so great is its fear of coming to consciousness. After all, what feminism both promised and threatened was a level of self-knowledge that would make it almost impossible to go on living with the old social agreements; that surely meant a rupture with God and country that millions found unbearable to even imagine. . . .

What none of us on my side of the divide understood was how primitive these issues actually were, and how far-reaching was both the fear—and, yes, the despair—they induced, even in the most unlikely of people. I myself had an abortion during these years and was shocked to see that in the days following the procedure I walked around feeling haunted by a sense of dread I could not account for, as though I had done that for which I would be punished. I realized then that if I, secular to the bone, could find myself in spiritual turmoil after an abortion, the true believer must undergo great terror at the mere thought of it. The experience did not temper my own activism on behalf of legal abortion, but it did temper my outrage. I could even feel in the right-to-lifers the anxiety, the panic, the oppressive sense of a world turned upside down—all that makes one blind to sweet reason—and then I felt the dismay of sorrow more than the energizing blaze of anger. I knew that the gulf between us was going to grow ever wider as the years progressed, and that as it did, the so-called fabric of American life would begin seriously to fray. Countless societies had been here times without number, and the outcome has always been up for grabs.

2017

# MERVE EMRE
# TWO PATHS FOR THE PERSONAL ESSAY



The first time I read Merve Emre was in the pages of *Boston Review*. It was an essay about the personal essay, the much-maligned form that has been declared dead more than once yet seems to be just as popular as ever, its various iterations marching across the web like some undead army. So even though Emre's essay was published eight years ago, it still reads like a much-needed rout of all those articles that proliferate on our feeds. It is a call for clarity and rigor, and an argument against sentimental self-exploration and being so much in our feelings, told with lancing wit and enviable erudition. She sees the great Mary Gaitskill as an antidote to the moral and aesthetic flabbiness of the modern personal essay, and praises her thusly: "For her reader, it feels refreshing to finally have a grownup in the room." One could say the same of Emre, as well as the magazine that published her.

**—Ryu Spaeth, features editor at *New York* magazine**

**UNDER WHAT CONDITIONS** should we care about the stories of other peoples' lives? Why, especially, should we care about them as works of art? I think there is a lesson to be learned in recalling the barest definition of "care": "To feel concern (great or little), trouble oneself, feel interest." Nowhere does it specify what the character of care must be; how hot or how cold it must run to do some good in the world. One can, as [Deborah] Nelson has, build a very persuasive case for compassion that is based on thoughtfulness, particularity, intellectual honesty—a more persuasive case, even, than compassion based on the boundlessness of feeling.

What is true for human relationships is true for art and politics. If I care about building a world, real or imaginary, with you or for you, then I should think about that world in the most accurate and realistic terms possible. I should hold you to the same standards of precision that I hold myself; even—and especially—if we disagree; even—and especially—if that disagreement is uncomfortable and alienating. "Something happens and we retell it as a story, preparing it for communication or for reviewing it later with oneself," Nelson writes. "Thoughtlessness begins with a deliberate choice not to represent actions in language, not to create memory." The refusal to represent, or the insistence on representing messily, is a refusal to share the world with others; a turn away from reality that is comforting because it is so deeply self-absorbed.

This brings us back to the personal essay. More than a fad and more than a form, we might think of the personal essay as a contract between reader and writer. The contract is not necessarily an emotional or intimate one, but, like all contracts, it is mutually constructed and it demands clarity. Just as the writer commits her imperceptible acts of cognition to language, asking the reader to accept this language as a poor proxy for her inner life, so too does the reader acknowledge and participate in this fantasy of self-construction. Together, reader and writer act as co-creators of a new fictional persona, the knowing self. This task is impossible, or at least impossible to derive pleasure from, without particularity and concreteness—a sense of reciprocity and respect....

What we see in many personal essays today is not the shattering of language but the shattering of a pact. All we can hope for now is its speedy restoration.

# OLÚFẸ́MI O. TÁÍWÒ
## IDENTITY POLITICS AND ELITE CAPTURE



In the summer of 2020, we needed a new way to think about identity politics, one that could acknowledge both the immense possibilities of what was happening in the streets of America while also warning about how it all might be rerouted into something much safer. Táíwò's essay, "Identity Politics and Elite Capture," detailed how identity politics, which had started as a way for queer Black women to participate in protest movements, many of which excluded and discriminated against them, had been repurposed—forcefully and against the wishes of its intellectual creators—into a decadent and sclerotic linguistic tool mostly used to settle scores and advance careers within the elite spaces of corporate America, the academy, and the media. What I've always appreciated about Táíwò's work is that he has never fallen into cynicism or easy invective like many of those who have repurposed his critique to dismiss all liberation movements or to sneer at anything smelling of "idpol," but rather has been resolute in his original reclamation project in the pages of *Boston Review*: "in the end, we're in it together—and, from the point of view of identity politics, that is the whole point."

**—Jay Caspian Kang, staff writer at *The New Yorker***

**INSTEAD OF FORGING ALLIANCES** across difference, some have chosen to weaponize identity politics, closing ranks—especially on social media—around ever-narrower conceptions of group interests rather than building solidarity. Identity politics itself isn't at fault. The trouble is that, like so many other things, identity politics is the victim of elite capture—deployed by political, social, and economic elites in the service of their own interests, rather than in the service of the vulnerable people they often claim to represent.

The concept of elite capture originated in the study of developing countries to describe the way socially advantaged people tend to gain control over financial benefits meant for everyone, especially foreign aid. But the concept has also been applied more generally to describe how political projects can be hijacked—in principle or in effect—by the well positioned and resourced. The idea also helps to explain how public resources such as knowledge, attention, and values get distorted and distributed by our power structures. And it is precisely what stands between us and Barbara Smith's urgent vision of coalitional politics.

A key problem with elite capture is that the subgroup of people with power over and access to the resources that get used to describe, define, and create political realities—in other words, elites—are substantively different from the total set of people affected by the decisions they make. As the part of the group closest to power and resources, they are typically the part whose interests overlap with the total group's the least. In the absence of the right kind of checks or constraints, they will capture the group's values, forcing people to coordinate on a narrower social project than the group would if power were distributed differently. When elites run the show, the "group's" interests get whittled down to what they have in common with those at the top. . . .

If elite capture boils down to the way power and resources tend to be distributed within groups, and not simply across groups, then it is a fully general problem of politics in a world that distributes power and resources unjustly and unequally. Elites get outsize control over the ideas in circulation about identities by, more or less, the same methods and for the same reasons that they get control over everything else.

2021

# WILLIAM CALLISON & QUINN SLOBODIAN

## CORONAPOLITICS FROM THE REICHSTAG TO THE CAPITOL



Nine months into the COVID-19 pandemic, with politics going haywire in all kinds of ways, *Boston Review* published "Coronapolitics from the Reichstag to the Capitol" by William Callison and Quinn Slobodian. It was the first major piece of analysis that succeeded in making real sense of the ways that conspiratorial fantasies about the virus were scrambling political signals across the political map. Surveying anti-lockdown coalitions that included far-right parties, wellness gurus, and entrepreneurial activists, they coined the term "diagonalism" to describe these emergent alliances. Their original framing helped many of us to understand the ways that pandemic-era conspiracy culture has carried the far right to terrifying heights in country after country. It's timely and rigorous work like this that makes *Boston Review* indispensable.

**—Naomi Klein, activist and author of *The Shock Doctrine***

LED IN MANY CASES by angry freelancers and the self-employed, amplified by entrepreneurs of speculative and totalizing prophecies, these movements are less what José Ortega y Gasset called "the revolt of the masses" and more "the revolt of the Mittelstand"—small- and medium-sized businesses. In comparison to the populism that dominated discussion in 2017, they are less tethered to mediagenic leaders and parties, slipperier on the traditional political spectrum, and less fixated on the assumption of state power. . . .





At the extreme end, diagonal movements share a conviction that all power is conspiracy. Public power cannot be legitimate, many believe, because the process of choosing governments is itself controlled by the powerful and is de facto illegitimate. This often comes with a dedication to disruptive decentralization, a desire for distributed knowledge and thus distributed power, and a susceptibility to right-wing radicalization. Diagonal movements trade in both familiar and novel fantasies about elite control. They attack allegedly "totalitarian" authorities, including the state, Big Tech, Big Pharma, big banks, climate science, mainstream media, and political correctness. They are, in many ways, descendants of the extra-parliamentary New Social Movements of the 1970s but with the idealism and desire for collective action or decommodification burned down to the wick of a defense of autonomous decision-making.

It would be easy to dismiss such mobilizations as manifestations of conspiratorial thinking, morbid symptoms of a morbid year with the United States acting as a "superspreader" of distrust, as one source told the *Washington Post*. But as the cultural theorist Jeremy Gilbert recently pointed out, "conspiracy theory" has many of the failings of the earlier category of "populism": it is too often used prematurely to foreclose a form of politics as illegitimate and, by othering it, can grant it the mark of martyrdom its followers seek.

An old axiom of political science dictates that governments rule by "carrots, sticks and sermons"—that is, coercion and incentive but also information. Diagonalism reminds us that universal internet access, the attention-absorbing power of social media platforms, and the dynamics of "incitement capitalism" have left the state's official script ragged with perforations and made space for hostile counterpublics, agents of "disinfotainment," social movements of rabbit holes, gig conspiracies for the gig economy. We have no choice but to wade in.

Image: Lori Hiris

# CREATURES APART

*Vivian Gornick*

*Airless Spaces*
Shulamith Firestone
Semiotext(e), $17.95 (paper)

WHEN I WAS a girl in the 1950s women, for the most part, got married, gave birth, and stayed home; if necessary, they went to work as schoolteachers or secretaries or salesgirls. They did not enter the professions, start a business, serve in government, or become university professors; nor did they climb a telephone pole, go down in the mines, or compete in a marathon. Today a girl is born with the knowledge that not only can she do any or all of the above, it is even assumed that she will pursue a working life as well as a domestic one. The change in social expectations for women, nothing short of monumental, is due to the Second Wave of American feminism (otherwise known as the Women's Liberation Movement), a political and social development characterized by the twin efforts of liberals who worked throughout the 1960s, '70s, and '80s to achieve equality for women under the law and radicals who worked to eradicate deep-dyed, historic sexism through a change in cultural consciousness. Among the leading figures in this second group was Shulamith Firestone, of whom it was said, "I think of her as a shooting star. She flashed brightly across the midnight sky, and then she disappeared." That's exactly how I remember her.



Although I, too, was a Second Wave feminist, I functioned in the Movement more as a writer than a group-oriented activist. In fact, I first met Shulamith when I interviewed her for my first feminist piece for the *Village Voice*. I can still see her that day in 1969, sitting in the kitchen of her fourth-floor Lower East Side walk-up—small, fierce, large dark eyes peering out at me from the middle of that extraordinary mane of waist-length black hair—answering my every question with the rapid-fire rhetorical skill that marked her every utterance. It was no surprise to me when, the following year, her first book, *The Dialectic of Sex: The Case for Feminist Revolution* was published and I, along with the rest of the world, felt the full force of her Talmudic brilliance. What was a surprise was how quickly after the book's publication she seemed to disappear from feminist politics, not to be heard from again (publicly, that is) until *Airless Spaces*—a work as shockingly concrete as *Dialectic* had been magisterially theoretical—was published in 1998, and the world also learned of how tormented the years in between had been for Shulamith. Now, *Airless Spaces* is being published anew, and having read it again for the first time in all these years, I am again amazed to feel the remarkable strength of mind and spirit with which Shulamith greeted every experience that life threw at her.

---

**SHE WAS BORN** in Ottawa, Ontario, in January of 1945 into a family of Orthodox Jewish Americans, then raised in St. Louis, Missouri. The father was a domestic tyrant, a man of raging righteousness who governed with an iron hand; but Shulamith, the second child in a brood of six, proved more than a match for him, defying his arbitrary rule from earliest life, possessed as she was of a temperament much like his own. Very young, Shulamith felt the unfairness inherent in having been born female. Once, during her teenage years, her father commanded her to make her brother's bed; when she asked why she must do this, she was told, "Because you're a girl," whereupon Shulamith flew into a rage of such severity one of her sisters thought that either she would murder their father or he would murder her.

She thought incessantly about the cultural subordination that doomed a woman to a life of secondary experience, and she read, read, read—Marx, Freud, Beauvoir—applying all she learned to this problem, concluding quite early that what women needed was a theory of sexual domination equal to that of class theory itself. As her ideas clarified, so too did her single-minded, almost visionary concentration on how to bring about organized protest on behalf of women's rights.

In September 1967, along with two thousand other New Left activists, Shulamith attended the National Conference for New Politics in Chicago. Here, she met Jo Freeman, already an activist on behalf of women, and together they crafted a resolution demanding equitable marital and property laws, control by women of their own bodies, and a 51 percent representation of women on the conference floor. When they, together with a few other budding feminists, approached the conference director with the request that their resolution be added to the agenda, he laughed. "Cool down, little girl," he said, actually patting Shulamith on the head. "We have more important things to talk about than women's problems." The women repaired to Freeman's apartment and there and then the first women's liberation group in Chicago was formed. A month later Shulamith moved to New York, where she quickly helped found two of the earliest and most important movement groups—New York Radical Women, which invented consciousness raising, and Redstockings, which concentrated on history from a feminist perspective. Months later, she also helped found New York Radical Feminists, by which time similar groups had begun to sprout across the entire country, and within the year the Women's Liberation Movement was born.

Shulamith's superior intelligence in combination with her inflamed temperament made her an instant take-charge person in whatever group she joined or helped form; this also made her a person both revered and resented. In the late Sixties, she was often experienced in her women's groups first as a leader of great command and then as an autocratic power seeker. Whatever the political vicissitudes of her life, no one could separate Shulamith from her need to go on thinking about women's historic subordination or her determination to organize those thoughts into a written document. In 1970 she published *The Dialectic of Sex*, and with it made cultural history.

*The Dialectic of Sex* essentially posits that woman's subordinate place in virtually every cultural development from time immemorial can be traced to her role as the childbearer of the race. This unfortunate assignment by nature, Shulamith argued, has determined woman's entire history: from it all else flows. Her solution to the problem? An extremity of test tube babies. Let most if not all children be not only conceived but brought to term *outside the female body*. This alone will end women's oppression.

The book landed like a bombshell, first in America, then very soon across much of the world. Aside from the analysis itself, what was revolutionary here was the ferocity with which Shulamith argued her case, admitting to all its emotional impediments but urging that we nonetheless rise above sentimentality. She called childbirth "barbaric" and viewed the nuclear family as a stifling influence on the full, free development of an individual's inner life. In its depth, breadth, and severity, *The Dialectic of Sex* was both thrilling and dismaying. Before long, Shulamith Firestone was something of an international celebrity.

That was 1970. By then, she had already begun to withdraw from movement politics: she no longer wished to be a professional feminist. She retreated to her tenement apartment in the East Village and concentrated on drawing and painting (she had considerable talent as a visual artist). We will never know what her other future might have held, though, because something especially menacing was waiting in the wings—and very soon it came for her.

In the mid-1980s Shulamith was diagnosed with paranoid schizophrenia. From then until her death, a good twenty-five years later, an unimaginable amount of mental misery was hers to endure.

Life became an endless round of medication and madness: periods of lucidity alternating with periods of soul-destroying paranoia which led to repeated—and dreaded—incarcerations in mental hospitals. There were times when Shulamith starved because she was convinced her food was poisoned, times when she begged on the street because she thought she was penniless, times when she neither answered the door or the phone for weeks on end or, alternately, adopted elaborate disguises before she'd emerge from the hovel her apartment had come to resemble.



**Almost every tale has a different narrator but somehow they are all Shulamith—and they all end with a human soul, already in torment, feeling ever more diminished.**

Throughout all this she was neither forgotten nor abandoned; a changing but ever-faithful band of friends, comrades, and relatives routinely intervened to save her from herself, making sure the rent was paid, there was food in the refrigerator, and she was taking her medication. However, a mental patient, like an alcoholic, is endlessly cunning when it comes to subverting salvation, and Shulamith Firestone was one of the best. Nothing could stop her from unraveling. One day in August 2012, when she was sixty-seven years old, she was found dead, face-down on the floor of her shabby, broken-down apartment. It was estimated that she'd been dead for either some days or some weeks.

The remarkable thing was that she had never stopped working. Throughout those terrible years of intermittent insanity, she wrote, she painted, she drew. When she died she left behind at least one complete novel, hundreds of poems and stories, many paintings and drawings. Most of it never got published or exhibited but there it was, a testament to a mind and spirit that refused to be extinguished before the body in which they were housed stopped functioning.

The problem, always, was the medication she was forced to take: on the one hand, it subdued her paranoia; on the other, it left her feeling like a zombie. Shulamith on meds was a quiet person without one interesting thought in her head; Shulamith off meds was brilliant and uncontrollable. Robert Roth, a friend throughout the years, has written about Shulamith and her Jekyll-Hyde relationship to her prescribed drugs: "I would know early on when she went off her medication. Weeks before the full effects would surface, very sharp, shimmering perceptions would flash out. . . . They were so vivid and poetic. Like a sudden burst of light breaking through thick, dense clouds. . . . That's when we knew trouble was ahead."

Roth also writes of "the immense responsibility falling on friends and family. . . . To let her die. Be injured. Not let her die. Become her jailor." To hospitalize her was to "betray her" by letting the institution "put a chemical lock on her emotions, her creativity." Even worse, it was to condemn her to a terrible aloneness. "Without community it is all so horrible."



In a 2024 issue of *And Then*, a magazine of contemporary writing which Roth helps edit, there appears a three-page poem of Shulamith's. Written sometime in the 1980s or 90s, the poem—called "Vending in the Street"—delivers wonderfully on the flavor of Shulamith's life when she was off medication but not yet hospitalized. The narrating perspective is that of someone who's become financially derelict but the voice delivers a shocking evocation of what it means, existentially speaking, to find oneself in social freefall. Here's a bit of it:

> hitting bottom
> *there is no bottom*
>
> I thought I could sink no lower
> than to sell
>     slush
> in the streets of Manhattan
> in august
>
> But I was wrong!
> [. . . ]
> *at bottom*
> *there is no bottom*
>
> I thought I could sink no lower
> than to pass out on the floor

at the health department
after waiting 3 days
in the 6 a.m. line
for a vendor's license

but I was wrong!
[. . . ]
I thought I could sink no lower
then tussling with a crippled
black beggar
who had stolen my (illegal) panhandling
  site
at the subway entrance
in front of may department stores

but I was wrong!
I could be busted
(handcuffs and all)
for returning to that site
after being warned by the cops
never to panhandle there again.

*at bottom*
*there is no bottom*

At bottom there is no bottom. This from the woman who wrote *The Dialectic of Sex*.

---

**SOMETIME IN THE 1990S** Shulamith was persuaded to pull together a number of the short pieces she had written that were strewn about the apartment, most of them an outgrowth of her repeated hospitalizations. A friend with a connection took the manuscript to the independent book publisher Semiotext(e), where it was immediately accepted and published in 1998 as a book of short stories.

Except "stories" seems not quite the right word for the collection, which reads far more like a group of journal entries. Most of the pieces are very short, not more than a page or so, and almost all feel like a fragment of thought abandoned before it could be shaped into a reading experience. Nonetheless, as a whole, the book is strangely powerful. I read it in a single sitting and then, feeling both gripped and dissatisfied, went through it again, this time tagging, here and there, a line I'd found striking. When I turned the last page I typed the lines out, one beneath the other, as in a laundry list, and read them again. Lo and behold, I found my heart pressing against my chest. A woman gifted with a significant intellect and an urgent need to right a historic wrong loses the ability to ground herself in everyday rationality—and writes a book that captures the situation so graphically it elevates her condition to the status of metaphor. *The Dialectic of Sex* is a polemic. *Airless Spaces* is literature.



---

**THE BOOK IS DIVIDED** into a number of sections—Hospital, Post-Hospital, Losers, Obits, and Suicides I Have Known—the most important of these being the first two. The pieces here, as Chris Kraus explains in the new edition's introduction, do not so much relate the history of Shulamith's own mental illness as provide Shulamith with the opportunity to embed her reader in the penetrating experience of institutionalization. Almost every tale has a narrator with a different name and a different identity but somehow they are all Shulamith—and they all end with a human soul, already in torment, feeling ever more diminished as the episodes accumulate and the environment thickens. Ultimately, what *Airless Spaces* is recording is the gradual shriveling of the human spirit when subjected to the practices of a social system that cannot help but equate obedience with mental health.

And now we're into it:

In one piece a terrified patient has refused to bathe for quite some time. When at last she is pushed under the shower, the experience is deadly. She is held down by four people (one for each limb), scrubbed mercilessly, her legs forced apart, her hair attacked not with shampoo but with some vile cleansing liquid, all of which leaves her feeling violated. Worse: "From this time on Corinne began to look like a mental patient, not an attractive woman who just happened to be thrown into a mental hospital." This is one of a number of times in *Airless Spaces* when the reader is made to feel the sense of loss that comes with the slow, steady erasure of oneself as a sexual person—a routine experience in the hospital.

Then there is Bettina, who "[has] severe insomnia and the loveless hospital only made it worse." Her entire body hurts and she often feels like she is about to jump out of her skin. When the endless wakefulness becomes unbearable, "that is right before the blood test teams came in and the morning shift changed, somewhere in the hour of the wolf," Bettina, like the wounded animal that she is, "[takes] to circling around her bed and counting." It is this circling and counting, which alone soothes her, that is held against Bettina when her evaluation hearings are held.



**Loneliness is at the heart of *Airless Spaces.* Mental illness is the metaphor of choice, but the author has something more encompassing on her mind.**

Next we have a woman who is released and yet not released from the hospital (as was Shulamith herself on a number of occasions). It seems she had left her apartment in an uninhabitable state and now, while it is being put to rights, the hospital insists on housing her in a room at the Y, where her sense of isolation becomes ever more acute: "She waited all week and a half for her one hour social work visit, her only contact with humanity," and the reader wonders, why her only contact with humanity? There are residents and staff workers and visitors at the Y, but the patient spends her days and nights as though in solitary confinement. Why? The aloneness is morbid: she herself is aware of how odd is her own conviction that the human touch is permanently beyond her reach. But then again, her sense of life among others had, in fact, been coming apart from the moment the hospital doors had closed behind her. Now she is being told it's not just because of the apartment that she cannot be fully released, it's that she must enter a day program where she will be instructed to meet and mingle with new people. On the instant life has become a Catch-22. She has a horror of these programs. She is convinced that if she enters one she'll be stigmatized as a permanent patient: she'll never again get a job or if she gets one she won't hold it. Of course, it isn't a job she won't be able to get or hold—but nothing can persuade her otherwise.

Another first-person narrator tells us that she's "read of a Reichian treatment once which was deemed successful"—a seventy-nine-year-old woman receiving it began to recover from cancer—but, the narrator thinks to herself, she's alone in the world, she's got no one and nothing to go home to, so what good is the medical reprieve? The implication for the reader: that's what's waiting for each of us, when we get out of here. We are all homeless, permanently homeless, irremediably homeless, homeless within ourselves.



In the bluntly titled "Hating Hospitals," Shulamith, through one of her surrogates, tells us that there are a number of ways a person can enter a psychiatric ward, chief among them either voluntarily or involuntarily. A self-styled free spirit, she has "always made a point of going in as involuntary—wheelchairs, police breaking in the door (sometimes up to ten men at once), EMS ambulances and police cars, handcuffs and injections, the whole bit." She knows this style of resistance is ultimately self-defeating—her involuntary status will be held against her when she applies for release and moreover, "it was a sure ticket to second-class status inside the hospital itself"—but she feels obligated, "just for honor's sake," to register her refusal to cooperate with a system that protects itself at the expense of one's innate dignity.

---

**A FOUNDING MYTH** tells us that after Adam and Eve ate of the Tree of Knowledge they evolved into beings endowed with consciousness, and from then on they were creatures apart, no longer at one with all the dumb animals with whom they had previously shared the Earth. The gifts of thought and emotion left the human race feeling both proud and lonely. The loneliness proved our undoing. It so perverted our instincts that we became strangers to ourselves—the true meaning of alienation—and thus creatures unable to feel kinship with others.

This *ur*-loneliness is at the heart of *Airless Spaces*. Mental illness is the metaphor of choice, but the author has something more encompassing on her mind. Drifting around as she does, in a world of women and men who, for one reason or a thousand, are enveloped in an almost biblical sense of internal isolation, she, in episode after episode, makes the reader feel the ravages of an affliction which, very nearly, seems inborn. Perhaps, having been burdened with a psyche divided against itself, humanity is destined to live homeless, addicted, incarcerated; in which case it is incumbent on the self-policers among us to show mercy. **BR**

Image: Vesuvius Challenge

# PLATO AND THE POETS

*Elaine Scarry*

WHEN PLATO WAS an infant, bees alighted on his lips and, nestling there, set about making honey. His parents had placed him, sleeping, on the summit of a mountain while they paid tribute to the gods, and when they turned their attention back to him, they found the infant's mouth full of golden sweetness. Cicero provides our first surviving record of the legend, which is repeated with variations over centuries, always as a portent of the sweet style the infant would ultimately possess.

Plato's honeyed voice was celebrated in classical antiquity by thinkers as different as Aristotle, Cicero, and Diogenes Laertius. Praise for Plato's literary genius regularly recurs until at least the early nineteenth century. As the Romantic poet Percy Shelley writes, "Plato was essentially a poet—the truth and splendour of his imagery, and the melody of his language, are the most intense that it is possible to conceive."

So it is odd that Plato is now so often presented as the great enemy of poetry. It is true that in Book X of *The Republic*, narrated by Socrates, Plato does—famously—contemplate banishing the poets from his ideal city. This episode has become the principal point of reference for the now-conventional picture of Plato as poetry's adversary, a view widely held by the likes of classicists and philosophers, literary critics, and many thousands with a much lighter acquaintance with Plato. That's not to say the question doesn't continue to occasion fierce debate in certain circles: the more than two millennia of literature on Plato's relationship to poetry are far from settled. But over the last half-century, that scholarly nuance seems to have become partially eclipsed and replaced by an offhand, common-sense view that has hardened into dogma.



**Was Plato really hostile to poets? Or did he, rather, insist on the crucial importance of poetry to almost every subject he placed before us?**

Classicist Stephen Halliwell, protesting this misunderstanding, decries "the standard reading of Plato's supposedly outright 'hostility' to poetry and the tired, reductive slogan that Plato 'banished the poets.'" Held even by "acute readers" of Plato like philosophers Myles Burnyeat and Hans-Georg Gadamer, the view is described by Halliwell as a "bleak and I think mistaken modern orthodoxy." In a 2015 *New Yorker* article about Sappho, Daniel Mendelsohn writes that Plato "is said to have called [Sappho] the Tenth Muse." But lest there be any confusion, he adds that "Plato, whose attitude toward literature was, to say the least, vexed . . . thought most poetry had no place in the ideal state." And in a recent *New Yorker* piece, Agnes Callard agrees with interviewer Rachel Aviv when Aviv dismisses as "silly" some lines by Rainer Maria Rilke. This is "why Socrates thought the poets didn't know what they were talking about," Callard then adds.

Mendelsohn and Callard are devotees of both Plato and literature, and are cited here just to make visible the intractability of the position. Each offers a casual gesture, not because either takes Plato lightly (far from it), but because the point is now so uncontroversial and so familiar that nothing more is needed. Remember Plato? He was an enemy of the poets.

But was Plato really hostile to poets? Or did he, rather, insist on the crucial importance of poetry—imaginative, emotionally evocative, and able to provide access to cognitive powers otherwise unavailable—to almost every subject he placed before us? The stakes of the question are high for three reasons.

First, there is presumably a true answer and we ought to find out what it is. Alfred North Whitehead wrote that all European philosophy is "a series of footnotes to Plato." So as the footnotes keep coming, we should try to get the original right. But there are more practical concerns as well. Plato carries such weight that placing scorn for poetry in his voice misleads people into believing that they suffer no intellectual harm when they ignore poetry, as most citizens today do. Moreover, classrooms, countries, and international communities need great philosophy; cutting off philosophers from poetry's expressive resources—confining them to abstract, rational argument—sabotages their essential work. How, then, did Plato regard the poets? And what do we miss if we get the answer wrong?

---

**OVER THE COURSE** of his dialogues, Plato quotes Homer 150 times, with passages from all but one of the *Iliad*'s twenty-four books. Socrates and others in the dialogues who quote poetry do so from memory. Plato positions Socrates in competition with Homer, whose *Iliad* and *Odyssey*—recited by rhapsodes at the Panathenaea every fourth year—had a colossal civic presence. Sophocles, Euripides, Aeschylus, and Aristophanes placed their verse plays in competition each spring in the Great Dionysia Festival. Such contests conveyed a shared object of emulation, a realm of value and beauty each contestant aspired to occupy. Plato explicitly conjures forth such matches in his dialogues: the *Symposium* takes place on the day one of its participants, Agathon, has just received the city's prize for tragedy; in *Phaedrus*, Socrates seeks to show that he is a better rhetorician than Lysias, whose speeches Phaedrus at first holds in high regard; in *Ion*, Socrates proves himself a better rhapsode than Ion, who at the opening has just won a prize for recitation in another city.

Even dialogues that are not directly about the verbal arts often foreground Socrates's poetic genius. This is strikingly so in the four extraordinary dialogues that record the city's accusation against Socrates (*Euthyphro*), his trial (*Apology*), his imprisonment (*Crito*), and the night of his execution (*Phaedo*). Plato, according to Diogenes Laertius, intended the four to be read together as a tetralogy, "like those of the tragic poets."



These dialogues explore essential philosophical ideas. One, we have a duty of justice. As Socrates says in *Crito*, "Both in war and in the law courts and everywhere else you must do whatever your city and your country command, or else persuade it in accordance with universal justice." Two, we have an obligation to accept punishment from the state, founded on the doctrine of "tacit consent." By residing in a country, we in effect give our consent to its laws, which creates an obligation to obey. For this reason, Socrates in *Crito* refuses to accept his friends' pleas to escape to another land. And three, the demands of justice do not change as death nears. Socrates argues, again in *Crito*, that the principles of justice cannot be modified just because he has suffered "this accident" that is leading to his execution. As time runs out—as it did for Socrates—we should change the way we think about *death*, not about justice: "those who really apply themselves . . . to philosophy are . . . preparing themselves for dying and death," and "courage belongs primarily to the philosophical disposition," he declares in *Phaedo*. Where is the poet in the exploration of these philosophical ideas? Everywhere.

The four dialogues enact a verbal tour de force relentlessly yoked to poetry. In the *Euthyphro*, we learn that Socrates has been indicted for the acts of heresy and corrupting the youth. Among the many translations of the indictment, only Benjamin Jowett's names the real charge: "He brings a wonderful accusation against me, which at first hearing excites surprise: he says that *I am a poet* [emphasis added] or maker of gods, and that I invent new gods and deny the existence of old ones." Explaining the charge of heretical invention, Euthyphro says it is "because of your saying you are constantly visited by your supernatural voice." The significance of such visitation is not explained here, though it is directly linked with poetic inspiration in dialogues such as *Ion*, *Phaedrus*, *Crito*, and *Phaedo*. Instead, Socrates announces that he is descended from Daedalus, the great sculptor.

The fame of Daedalus arises from his making lifelike statues that appear to move. Both Socrates and Euthyphro remark that Socrates's verbal arguments and sentences are so lithe and nimble that they have this same aura of motion. The art that Daedalus carries out in material artifacts, Socrates and his interlocutors carry out in verbal artifacts. Socrates concludes playfully that he must then be "a greater genius in my art than Daedalus was; he only gave his own works the power of movement, whereas I apparently give it to other people's as well as my own." This framing of Socrates as the offspring of Daedalus is just the warm-up for the poetic honors Plato will eventually confer on him in the tetralogy.



In the *Apology*, after his conviction and death sentence, Socrates addresses himself not to the full jury of 501, but to the minority of 141 who voted against execution. He speaks to console them, or—as he puts it—to reconcile them to the result. They should not feel sorrow because one of two things is true: either there is no consciousness after death, in which case death will have the sweetness of a night of dreamless sleep; or instead, there will be consciousness after death in the immortal realm. Here is the way he describes the second alternative:

> If on the other hand death is a removal from here to some other place, and if what we are told is true, that all the dead are there, what greater blessing could there be than this, gentlemen? . . . Put it in this way. How much would one of you give to meet Orpheus and Musaeus, Hesiod and Homer? I am willing to die ten times over if this account is true.

Imagining an immortal realm where everyone who ever lived and died is present, Socrates assumes his listeners—and certainly he himself—would most like to speak with Homer, Hesiod, Orpheus, and Musaeus. Plato and Socrates considered these four among the greatest poets, as *Ion* and other dialogues make clear.

Now at this point—midway through the tragic tetralogy—a question has surely begun to arise in my reader's mind: How can the claim that Plato is opposed to poets possibly survive the inconvenient celebration they are accorded here in what are surely among the most important moments in Socrates's life? We can catch a glimpse of how this takes place by consulting some of the dialogues' most popular translations.

First is a Penguin translation by Hugh Tredennick, still in use today but altered from the version in wide circulation from the 1950s to 1993. That edition takes the sentence in the *Apology*— "How much would one of you give to meet Orpheus and Musaeus, Hesiod and Homer?"—and appends three footnotes to the names of these poets. The footnote for Orpheus reads: "*Orpheus* is no doubt mentioned not as a singer and a poet but as the founder of Orphism." Of Musaeus we learn that he "was a bard like Orpheus, but his benefactions consisted in giving oracles for the curing of disease." The note appended to Hesiod—less quick to sidestep

**Where is the poet in the exploration of these philosophical ideas? Everywhere.**

his poetry—says: "*Hesiod* of Ascra in Boeotia was the first didactic poet; he was generally ranked next after Homer in antiquity and merit." The fact that all four poets can be associated with instruction or revelation is a potentially illuminating point. But Tredennick's clear implication is that Socrates is excited to meet Musaeus, Orpheus, and Hesiod for some reason other than their poetry.

If problems posed by proper names can be so easily muted, one can appreciate how much more easily ordinary nouns and adjectives can be modified to eliminate any suggestion that Socrates or Plato revered poets and poetry. In *Ion*, the Greek word for "beauty" and "beautiful"—*kalos*, *kalè*, *kalon*—appears multiple times in close association with poetry: it is used to describe the best epics, the best lyrics, and the single best encomium. But *kalos* is sometimes (for example, in the translations by Lane Cooper and W. R. M. Lamb) rendered not by the word "beautiful" but instead by words such as "lovely," "splendid," or "fine"—all of which are accurate and acceptable translations for *kalos* but which sever it from the great philosophic matter embedded in beauty, a subject Plato elaborately addresses in *Phaedrus*, *Symposium*, and *Greater Hippias*.

The act of bypassing the word "beautiful" in a work like Ion that is exclusively about poetry makes it possible for scholars to believe the two realms are separate. So decoupled are beauty and art in the contemporary reception of Plato that Nickolas Pappas's otherwise brilliant article on "Plato's Aesthetics" in the *Stanford Encyclopedia of Philosophy* actually begins:

> If aesthetics is the philosophical inquiry into art and beauty (or "aesthetic value"), the striking feature of Plato's dialogues is that he devotes as much time as he does to both topics and yet treats them oppositely. Art, mostly as represented by poetry, is closer to a greatest danger than any other phenomenon Plato speaks of, while beauty is close to a greatest good. Can there be such a thing as "Plato's aesthetics" that contains both positions?



What is relevant is not just the explicit mentions of artworks and names of tragedians or poets, but the many times when a dialogue calls attention to its own artistry or congratulates Socrates on his moments of ecstatic transmission. If proper nouns can be altered through footnotes and key nouns can be given alternative translations, then affirmations of poetry that are only implicit have close to zero chance of surfacing. But we have taken our intermission—between the first two dialogues in the tetralogy, *Euthyphro* and *Apology*, and the second two, *Crito* and *Phaedo*—long enough.

In *Crito* and *Phaedo*, Plato takes this alliance between Socrates and poetry further, attributing to Socrates direct acts of poetic composition in plays, hymns, and fables, conferring on him the title of poet, and counseling his friends and followers that his most important and difficult-to-replace work on Earth was that of the poet.

In *Crito*, Socrates responds to the counsel that he escape by staging a play for Crito in which the Laws (ventriloquized by Socrates) scold Socrates for contemplating such an act. The Laws describe what a ludicrous piece of theater Socrates would carry out if he attempted to escape to Thessaly by "arraying [himself] in some costume or putting on a shepherd's smock or some other conventional runaway's disguise." But the delight here is that the Laws announce this repudiation of theatrical escapades from *within* a piece of theater: Socrates's act of throwing his voice into the Laws, and thereby personifying and materializing them. The ventriloquism, an act of poesis, conveys a literal truth. When we consent to the rule of law, we throw our voices into the law and animate it; when we break the law, we take life from it.

Socrates's mimesis of his conversation with the Laws is framed by two mystical events that begin and end the dialogue. *Crito* opens with Socrates reporting his dream to Crito: "I thought I saw a gloriously beautiful woman dressed in white robes, who came up to me and addressed me in these words: 'Socrates . . .'" And here she begins to recite Homer in lines that Socrates interprets as predicting the timing of his execution.

By the end of *Crito*, the figures of the Laws and of the visionary female presence have converged. Socrates says: "That, my dear friend Crito, I do assure you, is what I seem to hear [the Laws] saying, just as a mystic seems to hear the strains of music, and the sound of their arguments rings so loudly in my heard that I cannot hear the other side." As Socrates externalizes his vision in the drama of the Laws, so the law is brought within him in the female dream figure and the music of the mystic ringing in his ears.

The bond between philosopher and poet reaches a climax in *Phaedo*, where Socrates's puzzled friends find him in prison on the eve of his execution. He is composing a hymn to Apollo and an adaptation of Aesop into verse. "In the course of my life," Socrates explains, "I have often had the same dream, appearing in different forms at different times, but always saying the same thing, 'Socrates, practice and cultivate the arts.'" He further explains that "because philosophy is the greatest of the arts, and [he] was practicing it," he had always believed himself to be in compliance. But ever since the trial, he has worried "it might be this popular form of art the dream intended me to practice, in which case I ought to practice it and not disobey."

Here, on the eve of death, Socrates fully embraces poetry. The play he staged in *Crito* was a stately piece of political philosophy. But here in *Phaedo*, the poetry is an overtly fictional fable. Socrates emphasizes this fictionality when he explains why he turned from hymn to fable:

> When I had finished my hymn, I reflected that a poet, if he is to be worthy of the name, ought to work on imaginative themes, not descriptive ones, and I was not good at inventing stories. So I

> availed myself of some of Aesop's fables which were ready to hand and familiar to me, and I versified the first of them that suggested themselves.

Socrates's disclaimer that he is not good at invention and must therefore piggyback on Aesop's ingenuity reminds us that what originally prompted his friends' inquiry about his poems was his on-the-spot invention of a fable and his judgment that Aesop would have offered the fable to the world, had he only thought of it:





> Socrates sat up on the bed and drew up his leg and massaged it, saying as he did so, What a queer thing it is, my friends, this sensation which is popularly called pleasure! It is remarkable how closely it is connected with its conventional opposite, pain. They will never come to a man both at once, but if you pursue one of them and catch it, you are nearly always compelled to have the other as well; they are like two bodies attached to the same head. I am sure that if Aesop had thought of it he would have made up a fable about them, something like this—God wanted to stop their continual quarreling, and when he found that it was impossible, he fastened their heads together; so wherever one of them appears, the other is sure to follow after. That is exactly what seems to be happening to me. I had a pain in my leg from the fetter, and now I feel the pleasure coming that follows it.

Even before Socrates composes his new Aesopian fable, he is already working as a fabulist by picturing us racing after either pleasure or pain, successfully grabbing hold of one, only to find we are also holding the other in our hands.

---

**THE THREE GENRES** that Socrates composes in *Apology* and *Phaedo*—play, hymn, and fable—occur throughout Plato's dialogues.

As in theater we are used to "the play within the play," so many of Plato's dialogues contain a dialogue within a dialogue: Socrates ventriloquizes Diotima's school of love (*Symposium*), Phaedrus re-enacts the speech of Lysias (*Phaedrus*), Socrates reports the way an "insolent" man challenged his ideas about beauty (*Greater Hippias*).

Hymns of praise to the gods recur in dialogues like *Critias* and *Laws*, and a palinode to the gods for having misspoken takes place when Socrates in *Phaedrus* explicitly offers his elaborate speech on love to make amends for earlier having impiously argued that the nonlover is better for Phaedrus than the lover.





The dialogues are saturated with fables as well. The *Symposium* contains Aristophanes's fable about the division of spherical humans into two hemispheres longing to reunite, a fable that has no known source in the comic playwright outside of this dialogue. Sometimes, to be sure, Plato's mythmaking may seem decorative: *Phaedrus* tells the entrancing story about the ceaseless songs of the cicadas. Often, however, it delivers the central philosophic idea—the myth of the cave in the *Republic*, the charioteer with his white and black horses in *Phaedrus*, and the ladder of love in the *Symposium*. Poetic devices—plays-within-plays, praise poems, and fables—are, then, as Platonic as his metaphysical theory of the forms.

**Poetic devices are as Platonic as his metaphysical theory of the forms.**

How, then, is Plato's immense admiration for poetry—and not just admiration, but powerfully poetic philosophical writing—denied in the face of such relentless affirmations? Perhaps because the tetralogy recounting the conviction and death of Socrates comprises early Platonic dialogues, before Plato turned against poetry. This explanation has the weakness that the highest number of references to poetry occur in the *Laws*, among the last of Plato's works. This inconvenient reminder generates a new explanation: poetry saturates the *Laws* because it is about the real state, not the *Republic*'s ideal state, and alas, there's no way to get rid of poetry in reality. And if a commitment to poetry is found to saturate a middle dialogue—as Martha Nussbaum's virtuosic analysis of *Phaedrus* demonstrates—it can be attributed to a sudden change of heart. As quickly as Plato's commitment to poetry is swatted down, it rises up again. Early, middle, and late dialogues: Plato's affirmations of poetry are everywhere.

Perhaps the most powerful affirmation comes at the close of the *Phaedo*. The subject is death. With death for Socrates just an hour or so away, the arguments about why we should not fear it seem unconvincing to his friends. You know, Socrates, one of them says, even after all your arguments, "there is a child within us to whom death is a sort of hobgoblin; him too we must persuade not to be afraid when he is alone with him in the dark." Socrates matter-of-factly provides the remedy to this seemingly remediless terror: "Let the words of the charmer be applied daily until you have charmed him away." The friend replies, in a sentence that must alter the heartbeat of many readers, "And where shall we find a good charmer of our fears, Socrates, when you are gone?"

Socrates counsels them that they must search everywhere across familiar and unfamiliar civilizations—"seek for him among them all, far and wide"—because it is the most important thing they can do. They then resume their dialogue until the sun sets, the hemlock is provided, and Socrates gradually ceases to speak.

---

**WHY, THEN,** the great exception in the *Republic*? Why does Plato launch an assault on poetry in there? It is only one out of dozens of dialogues, but many people regard it as Plato's most important work. Is it truly an exception or does it, in the end, conform to the affirmation of poetry found in the other dialogues?

Throughout the *Republic*, Socrates acknowledges that "Homer is the greatest of poets and first of tragedy writers." He, Socrates, has always been "charmed" and "delighted" by—no, much more than that, he greatly loves—Homer: "I have always from my earliest youth had an awe and love of Homer, which even now makes the words falter on my lips." If, he tells Glaucon, they at last conclude they must banish the poets, they will only do so in the way a lover severs himself with great pain from a beloved.

But have the beloved poets been banished by the end of the *Republic*? There are five reasons why, despite the dialogue's threat to banish the poets from the ideal state (kallipolis, the beautiful city), we should recognize that, in fact, no such banishment takes place.

First, Plato's contemporaries would be acutely aware that while the perfect state might or might not evict the poets, one very imperfect state *had actually* evicted a poet: that city was Athens, and the poet was Socrates. Socrates had already been dead for some twenty years when the *Republic* was written. *Euthyphro*, *Apology*, and *Crito* are generally assumed to have been written close to the time of Socrates's death, and Phaedo closer in time to the *Republic*. Not only the death of Socrates, but Plato's insistence on Socrates's stature as a poet would be clear in the minds of early listeners and should be kept clearly in our own minds as we listen to him 2,400 years later.

Some of Socrates's criticisms of the poets mimic the charges leveled against him: impiety to the gods and reckless teaching that endangers the state. Other charges differentiate them. Socrates's punishment was amplified by his refusal to weep or lament his fate during his trial, while one of his harshest critiques of poets in the *Republic* is their surrender to agonized lamentation: he berates the mourning of Achilles for Patroclus and the mourning of Priam for Hector—scenes at the heart of the *Iliad*. Soldiers should not, in Plato's account, surrender to grief because they should not mentally absent themselves from battle, just as Socrates in refusing to surrender to sentiment during his trial, keeps his mind agile and alert to the philosophic battle.

Both the overlap and the difference bring to mind the earlier historical ousting of a "poet." While Socrates's critiques of the poets enable him to mount a comeback to his accusers, the fifth-century audience of the *Republic*—now seemingly being asked to assent to the banishment of poets—would be on guard, mindful of the catastrophic loss to the city that came with Socrates's own banishment. Perhaps the case for banishing poets would have been heard less as an affirmative recommendation and more as a cautionary tale about the ideal city.

A second reason for concluding that the poets are not banished, or banished for long, is that Plato is—at the very moment of writing the *Republic*—weaving a great, imaginative artwork, a philosophic dialogue dependent at key stations on mythmaking. His Myth of the Metals tells people that they are made of different stuff, which justifies their different social roles; the Myth of the Cave provides a vivid rendering of the ascent from ignorance to knowledge; and the Myth of Er, which we will come to soon, provides a picture of cosmic justice. The *Republic*'s ten books are saturated with similes and metaphors, all the while providing a vivid mimesis of human beings in conversation (when there are no human beings actually present). Perhaps we should regard Book X as a poetics according to which the *Republic* itself is written and which therefore makes the dialogue immune to its criticisms.

Simplifying his more complex argument, Plato offers at least two main criticisms of poetry. Wrongful poets err by producing a third-order imitation, an image of an image of fundamental reality. They re-enact the actions of mortal souls and states that are themselves re-enactments of the ideal forms of city and soul. Plato, in contrast, provides a second-order imitation, an image at only one remove from the ideal *polis* and ideal soul. The problem is not poetic images, but the distance from fundamental reality of the images of images that wrongful poets offer. In addition, wrongful poets try to obscure how vacant their subject matter is by the rhythmic seduction of poetic meter. Plato, in contrast, will here speak exclusively in prose (or as Aristotle noted, something between poetry and prose).





Third, even as he makes the case for expulsion, Socrates arranges for two avenues of reprieve and return—hypothetical avenues that, as the fourth and fifth reasons below will show, Plato then actualizes:

> Notwithstanding this [referring here to the ancient quarrel between philosophy and poetry], let us assure our sweet friend and the sister arts of imitation that if she will only prove her title to exist in a well-ordered State we shall be delighted to receive her—we are very conscious of her charms; but we may not on that account betray the truth. I dare say, Glaucon, that you are as much charmed by her as I am, especially when she appears in Homer?
>
> Yes, indeed, I am greatly charmed.
>
> Shall I propose, then, that she be allowed to return from exile, but upon this condition only—that she make a defence of herself in lyrical or some other metre?

Shortly before this passage, the *Republic* has Socrates explicitly fault "epic or lyric verse" for "allow[ing] the honeyed muse to enter," and by doing so, to displace the rule of "law and reason" with that of "pleasure and pain." Yet now it is that very honeyed voice of lyrical meter that is invited to make a defense. Socrates then offers a second avenue of reprieve, this time without meter:

> And we may further grant to those of her defenders who are lovers of poetry and yet not poets the permission to speak in prose on her behalf: let them show not only that she is pleasant but also useful to States and to human life, and we will listen in a kindly spirit; for if this can be proved we shall surely be the gainers I mean, if there is a use in poetry as well as a delight?
>
> Certainly, he said, we shall [be] the gainers.



Socrates's two proposals—even if only hypotheticals—open up a breathing space, a place of grace. Further, he places no time limit on these two avenues of reprieve. They need not happen before the dialogue ends, nor even before Athens disappears. But as it happens, we do not wait long before they arrive.

Fourth, no sooner have the poets been banished than the *Republic* concludes with its Myth of Er, which readers often ignore, dismiss as curiously at odds with the banishment, or disparage: Julia Annas, who has written extensively on Plato, describes it as "vulgar," "childish," even "lame and messy." But the Myth of Er—with one of our earliest references to the Pythagorean music of the spheres—indeed shows that the poetic mind can contribute to "the well-ordered state" and provide something "useful to States and to human life," the strong requirements Socrates stipulated.

Throughout the *Republic*, Plato argues that human souls will more easily become just if the state is just, and that the state will more easily achieve just arrangements if its inhabitants are just, a reciprocal influence explored in detail by Jonathan Lear. But what if something greater than soul or state, the cosmos itself, is not just? How will soul and state maintain their justness under a bent sky?

The Myth of Er provides an account of cosmic justice that offers three assurances of human justice. One assurance is provided by the marvel of the music of the spheres—"harmony" within both soul and state, we have earlier learned, is nearly identical with justice, and surely cosmic harmony will help to inspire it. A second assurance is the connection affirmed in the myth between one's life on earth and what happens in the afterlife: the just are rewarded with upward lift into a thousand years of heaven and the unjust with a downward fall into a thousand years of torment.

**Philosophy and poetry are distinct inventions. But each suffers by keeping the other at arm's length.**



The third and most needed assurance is not about the afterlife, but the beforelife. Early in the *Republic*, we learn that some of us are born to be potters, some weavers, and still others guardians of the city; how can it be just if some are born into wealthy circumstances and others are poor and others enslaved; some are of one gender, some of another? The *Republic* instructs that justice consists in playing the hand one has been dealt, that which "they have in their hands." The "original principle . . . at the foundation of the State" is to "practice . . . the thing to which his nature was best adapted." We have a just city when each of the three classes in the city—the classes of artisan-producers, warriors, and philosopher-rulers—does what its nature is best suited to. This harmony of parts, rooted in natural differences, is not only the principle of justness but also "the condition and the cause" of all the other virtues—wisdom, courage, and temperance. But what about the natural endowments themselves: What are we to make of the sheer fortuitousness of their distribution? How does justice address the sheer but fateful moral luck of being dealt the hand of a ruler or the hand of an artisan?

The Myth of Er, with its cosmic architecture—part rower's trireme, part weaver's loom, part musician's lute—is the answer. Over eternity, each person will come to occupy all possible positions on Earth. The position—whether this time as a guardian-ruler or next time as a carpenter, mason, or soldier—will be the combined result of chance and choice: chance, because a blindfolded lottery will dispassionately deal out to all souls the numerical position in which they get to choose their next lives; and choice, because each soul will, on the basis of their most recent life, choose the next incarnation from the remaining options.

The myth instructs the carpenter not to resent the more fortunate circumstance of the guardian ruler, since over time we each will have a turn at all those roles. We may strongly disagree with Plato about the importance of staying within one's own position: today we often take easy social mobility as a key criterion for measuring the justness of a particular country. Given, however, Plato's insistence on playing the hand one has been dealt, the Myth of Er is a liberating gift since it enables one to concentrate on excelling where one stands rather than endlessly striving for "improving" one's social location. This thought experiment illustrates the usefulness of poetic mythmaking to soul and state and thereby assures poets a permanent place in the beautiful city. The banishment edict does not even survive as long as the book in which it is announced.

A final reason we should recognize the survival of the poets is that the critique of poetry given in the *Republic* is directly challenged by the sequence of dialogues in which Plato places the work: *Republic*, *Timaeus*, *Critias*. In the *Republic*, the conversation among Socrates, Glaucon, Thrasymachus, and their companions does not take place in the present moment. It has already taken place "yesterday" and is being reported by Socrates to other friends not themselves named in the *Republic*. But they are named at the opening of *Timaeus,* where Socrates says he has done his part by describing the beautiful city. Timaeus and Critias (and one other, whom we eventually learn is Hermocrates) now must do theirs. All four dialogues (*Republic*, *Timaeus*, *Critias*, and that of Hermocrates, which might have been intended to appear in *Critias* or in an unwritten dialogue bearing Hermocrates's own name) are entries in a competition like those entered into by playwrights in the Great Dionysian Festival.

Many ancient commentators grouped the *Republic*, *Timaeus*, and *Critias* together. Modern scholars cast doubt on this alliance of the three dialogues, noting that the time of year appears to be different, with the *Republic* taking place on the Bendideia in late May and *Timaeus* and *Critias* taking place at the Panathenaea in midsummer. But recently, Nerea Terceiro Sanmartin has convincingly shown that *Timaeus* and *Critias* take place not at the Panathenaea but at a lesser festival for Athena, the Kallynteria, which comes two days after the Bendideia. The three dialogues are therefore temporally consistent.

When *Timaeus* opens, Socrates is asked to summarize what he said last night and he proceeds to sketch the *Republic*'s account of justice.

At the opening of *Critias*, after the astronomer Timaeus has closed his incandescent account of the creation of the world, we are about to hear Critias's account of the earliest Athenians. Critias asks for "indulgence" since any account of a human society will be judged more "severely" than a depiction (as in *Timaeus*) of the immortal realm because everyone has seen the former but no one the later.

Critias's description of *Timaeus*—as a narrative that more easily receives a generous reception than the one he is about to give—applies to Socrates's account in the *Republic*, which was of an ideal (not a real) city. Critias thereby suggests that a second-order imitation—an imitation of true reality—may not, after all, be superior to a third-order imitation of the imitation, but may instead garner our praise only because, having no experience of the ideal, we cannot easily critique a narrative about it.

If we turn back to the opening of *Timaeus*, we see that this challenge to the superiority of second-order accounts over third-order accounts has already been introduced by Socrates himself. Here he worries that however fine his recitation has been in the *Republic*, there is something missing: it is not "alive," he confesses; it has "no motion" (like a painting of an animal standing still rather than running). His picture, he says, would be better if he could show the ideal state once it goes to war (oh, like the banished *Iliad*?, we wonder).

Here at the opening of *Timaeus*, Critias reveals that the *Republic* provoked a sense of déjà vu. Once he regained his bearings, he realized that the city of the first Athenians, nine thousand years ago, conformed in every detail to Socrates's description of the ideal state, even though these earliest Athenians were real men and women. The story was told to him by his grandfather who heard it directly from his contemporary Solon, who wrote about it in a long poem. Solon is not a philosopher king but a Poet King, whose gifts in poetry, says Critias, would have equaled or surpassed the gifts of Homer and Hesiod, had he made it his central task.

With *Timaeus* and *Critias*, Plato places the *Republic* in a larger frame of artistic competition (with Socrates, Timaeus, and Critias as the competitors). Moreover, the priority of third-order poetic representations over second-order philosophical representations is acknowledged to be a possibility, and a more alive version of the Republic is reported to be available in a poem by the Poet-King Solon, who originated (or at least strongly supported, as Greg Nagy points out) the requirement that Homer's *Iliad* and *Odyssey* be recited at the Panathenaea.

Further, the *Republic*'s second critique of poetry—that its meter seduces us away from rational judgment—is challenged by Timaeus's account of the binding of mortal creatures. The Original Artificer gives the cosmos unity by an intricate, analogical binding of earth, air, water, and fire, as well as by mathematical ratios, but mortal creatures achieve unity only by an array of pegs that hold everything together. Whenever they are slightly or even greatly out of kilter, poetic meter is applied to bring them back into perfect alignment again. Meter repairs human souls.



So two of the most serious charges against poetry in the *Republic* each receive a serious challenge, and may be defeated altogether. The Kallynteria festival honored the goddess Athena by being a time of cleansing her temple. Conceivably Plato could have intended *Timaeus* and *Critias* as a palinode making amends for having spoken against poetry, much as Socrates in *Phaedrus* gives a palinode making amends for having spoken against love. An intellectual world bereft of poetry would be as damaged as one where the nonlover is preferred to the lover.

---

**THE CARELESS ADAGE** that Plato banished poetry should itself be banished. It is untrue. It wounds poetry by severing poetry from one of its greatest advocates. It wounds a public that disregards poetry by assuring them they suffer no deficit. And it deforms political philosophy by tempting its practitioners to steer clear of metaphor and myth, even when philosophy's greatest contributions demonstrate the importance of meter, metaphor, and myth to powerful thinking.

Is it just a coincidence that the single best known page in the last fifty years of philosophy is a metaphor? John Rawls wrote principally in the prosaic style of analytical philosophy. But his most memorable contribution is the veil of ignorance, a compelling image of how to reason about justice in a way that gives equal attention to the good of each person.

The case of Rawls is the rule, not an exception. Hobbes's *Leviathan* draws on a world-transforming metaphor drawn from the Book of Job:

the state is like the great sea monster who tames human pride. Well into his eighties, Hobbes himself translated the 16,000 lines of *The Iliad* from the ancient Greek (not to mention the twenty-four books of *The Odyssey*) and foregrounded, more prominently than any other translation before or since, the dissent of Achilles. It is far from a coincidence that he, being steeped in such literature, had among his first principles the following: "If men will not obey the law, what is it that can make them? An army, you will say. But what shall make the army?"



Even if we ignore Locke's Latin poems, we cannot ignore the stream of metaphors throughout his *Second Treatise of Government*—as when he distinguishes his conception of limited government from the absolutists who think "men are so foolish, that they take care to avoid what mischiefs may be done them by pole-cats, or foxes; but are content, nay, think it safety, to be devoured by lions." Rousseau wrote a bestselling novel, *Julie*, and a popular opera, *Le Devin Du Village*; and works like *Confessions*, *Emile*, and *The Social Contract* are regarded as literary as well as philosophic masterpieces. Kant's regard for the stature of aesthetic judgment is indicated by his decision to dedicate a treatise to the subject. Schiller urged that freedom was impossible without aesthetic education. The cascade continues through Hegel, Dewey, Sartre, Beauvoir, Wittgenstein.

Philosophy and poetry are distinct inventions. But each suffers by keeping the other at arm's length. The fates of philosophical and poetic understanding are intertwined. They have a single history.

---

**WE DON'T KNOW** whether Plato and Socrates have had the chance to converse in the afterlife with Homer, Hesiod, Orpheus, and Museus. But last year, new technology able to decipher a set of disintegrating papyrus scrolls—in such fragile condition that they were previously unable to be read—brought to light new elements of a biography of Plato's life and death written by the philosopher Philodemus. What they reveal, according to a philosopher who worked on the project, is that Plato is buried on the grounds of his Academy in Athens "in a garden in a private area, near the sacred shrine to the muses." **BR**

Image: Ariella Aïsha Azoulay

# IN SEARCH OF ARAB JEWS

*Samuel Hayim Brody*

*The Jewelers of the Ummah: A Potential History of the Jewish Muslim World*
Ariella Aïsha Azoulay
Verso, $44.95

*Three Worlds: Memoirs of an Arab-Jew*
Avi Shlaim
Oneworld Publications, $29.95

*When We Were Arabs: A Jewish Family's Forgotten History*
Massoud Hayoun
The New Press, $27.99

## I. The Hand and the Eye

**AROUND MY NECK** I wear a golden chain. From this chain, two pendants hang. One takes the form of the Hebrew letters *chet* and *yod*, which spell the word *chai*, "life," from which my middle name also derives. My mother gave me this *chai* for my bar mitzvah, and I still wear it nearly thirty years later.

The other pendant is more mysterious. No one in my family can recall who gave it to me, and I don't remember buying it. It takes the form of a stylized hand, and on it are inscribed three Hebrew words invoking divine protection. This object is known in the Jewish world as a *hamsa*, from the Arabic word for "five." Muslims call it the Hand of Fatima, and it is most associated today with the countries of North Africa. But the image of the open hand, as a symbol of protection and care, probably precedes both Judaism and Islam; it has been found in ruins and imagery from Babylonia to Greece. And what does the hand protect against? Whatever the provenance, the answer is always the same: the eye. Specifically, the *evil* eye. Against the hatred, envy, and resentment of good luck and blessings observed in the eye, cultures across the Mediterranean agree: it is the hand that shields and defends.

Ariella Aïsha Azoulay's recent book, *The Jewelers of the Ummah: A Potential History of the Jewish Muslim World* (2024), uses the *hamsa* as a section marker within chapters. But more than that, this massive text is itself a *hamsa*—a paean to the craftwork of her Algerian-Jewish and Palestinian-Jewish ancestors' hands and a rejection of an evil way of seeing. A curator, filmmaker, and scholar of visual culture, Azoulay has long been concerned with documenting, as she puts it here, "the *longue durée* of the Euro-American investment in the destruction of the Jewish Muslim world, of which Palestine is now the ultimate site of its genocidal violence." With this book she means to evoke, in the most intimate detail to date, the totality of that destruction, "in order to remember, imagine, and speculate on what a different form of sharing the world might have been and still might become today." Precisely for this investment in conjuring the past, however, and again like the *hamsa*, it is likely to be experienced by readers with a progressive, rationalistic, and materialist outlook as superstitious, romantic, perhaps even conservative. Azoulay knows this; these are the readers she most wants to challenge.





The book is structured as a series of addresses to living and dead family members, poets, and thinkers who have inspired or provoked her. (An early version of one of these letters, to the French historian Benjamin Stora, first appeared in these pages.) The epistolary form distinguishes Azoulay's work from other recent memoirs by authors whom others may identify as "Mizrahi" but who describe themselves as "Arab Jews," among them the Moroccan-Egyptian-Tunisian-American journalist and artist Massoud Hayoun, in *When We Were Arabs: A Jewish Family's Forgotten History* (2019), and the Iraqi-Israeli-British historian Avi Shlaim, in *Three Worlds: Memoirs of an Arab-Jew* (2023). Memoirs may seem uniquely suited to cut through this bewildering thicket of categories, each with its own affordances and constraints. They direct our focus to the experiences of individuals, families, and communities, regardless of theory or the abstract narratives of history; they say, *here's who I am, here's who we were*. Even so, Azoulay makes grand, controversial claims that deserve both appreciation and scrutiny.

*Mizrahi*, a Hebrew word meaning "Eastern," is used in the State of Israel to refer to Jews from Muslim-majority countries. Confusingly, it has widely come to replace the older term *Sephardi*, even though the latter traditionally means "Spanish" and has been used since medieval times to describe the Jews of the Iberian Peninsula, many of whom fled to the lands of the Ottoman Empire after their expulsion in 1492. It has never made much sense to describe the Jews of Iraq, for example—millennia-old communities with no connection to Spain or Portugal—as Sephardi. Nor does it make sense to describe Morocco as "east" of Germany. Instead, *Mizrahi* is an artifact of Israeli history, yoking together Jews with divergent histories in Tunisia, Yemen, and Iraq as they underwent similar experiences of immigration. But precisely because those experiences were so humiliating, the term has its opponents. In *The Arab Jews: A Postcolonial Reading of Nationalism, Religion, and Ethnicity* (2006), Yehouda Shenhav translates *Mizrahi* as "Oriental," succinctly capturing the affects and attitudes that he and other opponents hear in it.





**Memoirs direct our focus to the experiences of individuals, families, and communities, cutting through inherited and abstract categories; they say, *here's who I am, here's who we were.***

As an alternative, "Arab Jews" has a subversive quality. Although the term was used throughout the twentieth century by thinkers and politicians ranging from the Tunisian-Jewish writer Albert Memmi to Israeli prime minister Golda Meir, it was pioneered in its current sense by the Iraqi-Jewish intellectual Ella Shohat. The category should not be thought of as attempting to perform the same work as "Mizrahi," however. Most obviously, it does not purport to include Jews who identify as Kurdish, Turkish, Persian, Afghan, or Berber. Quite the contrary, its advocates appreciate it for its *non*-comprehensiveness, its power to particularize. Hayoun puts it this way: "Like my ancestors for as long as my family can remember, I am Arab. Of Jewish faith. I am not Sephardi or Mizrahi. . . . My family is not from east of somewhere. To us, where we are from in North Africa is not in an imagined East of an imagined West; it is the center of our world."

The subversive power of "Arab Jew" may not be obvious to readers in the United States, where any religious designation seems free to modify any ethnic term. There are Arab Christians and Arab Muslims, so why not Arab Jews—people whose ancestors belonged to Arab lands, spoke Arabic, listened to Arabic music, ate Arab food, shared Arab customs and attitudes, all while believing in the God of the Torah and keeping the Jewish commandments? A significant part of Azoulay's implicit argument is that history has repressed this possibility, especially through a narrative of ancient enmity between "Jews and Arabs." (Shenhav deems this "methodological Zionism," founded on "an epistemology where all social processes are reduced to national Zionist categories.") This conjunction—this *and*—does violence to complex realities and hybrid identities wherever it goes. Think of how many books and articles continue to be published about "Blacks *and* Jews," as if no one were both Black and Jewish.



"European Jews," by contrast, are never wrenched apart in this way—and this, of course, is often precisely what is meant by *Ashkenazi*, the complement, or foil, to *Sephardi* and *Mizrahi*. If the conjunction is motivated by a history of enmity, this exception for Europe is strange, to say the least. Was Europe not, for centuries, a land of hellish persecution for Jews, who were estranged as the ultimate Others? Is this not what we recall when we inventory the sins of antisemitism—the blood libel and the expulsions, the ghettoes and the disputations, the pogroms and the Holocaust? Why, then, does it sound so stilted and unnatural to say "Europeans *and* Jews"?

Shenhav's idea of "methodological Zionism" provides one possible answer. Pioneered by Jews who hailed from Central and Eastern Europe, Zionism has historically posited both that Jews are a Middle Eastern nation unto themselves and that the Jewish state is culturally and politically "Western," which in this framework is essentially to say, *civilized*. The tension can be smoothed over if one effectively defines Jewish history as European Jewish history, marginalizing the histories of Jews outside of Europe. Shenhav proposes that this is one reason why Arab Jews are so often portrayed as traditionally pious. European Jews can be secular because their identity is always already affirmed by Zionism; Arab Jews, by contrast, must be Jewish "religiously." The philosopher Lewis R. Gordon has written about feeling pressure, as a Black Jew, to wear a *kippah* to signify Jewishness, as if he did not have the same right as a white Jew to be secular.

Azoulay has a different proposal, which extends Shenhav's idea in a more radical direction. She uses the term "Muslim Jews," incorporating Islamic categories into the discussion of her Algerian ancestors. The *ummah* of her title, a term that roughly means "global Islamic community," is meant to capture the preeminence of Jews in jewelry-making and metalwork throughout the precolonial Islamic world.

This provocative term also suggests the possibility of a parallel category of "Christian Jews," something many readers would surely reject. Two considerations might lessen the appearance of contradiction. The first may be illustrated by an anecdote told by Jacques Derrida—like Azoulay, an Algerian Jew. In his 1995 funeral oration for his colleague, the Lithuanian-French philosopher Emmanuel Levinas, Derrida relates that they once attended a lecture by André Neher at the Congress of Jewish Intellectuals. At some point during the talk, Levinas turned to Derrida and said: "You see, he's the Jewish Protestant, and I'm the Catholic." The joke works by metonymy: "Protestantism" as biblical primacy versus "Catholicism" as the importance of mediating tradition. (Derrida, for his part, called himself a "Marrano of French Catholic culture," alluding to Spanish Jews who were forcibly converted to Christianity in the fourteenth and fifteenth centuries but secretly maintained Jewish practices.)

Second, there is the category "Judeo-Christian." The term continues to be used uncritically across the political spectrum: on the right it names a heritage that supposedly undergirds Western civilization, while on the left it denotes the force that dispossesses the indigenous, represses the feminine, and despoils the earth. It has become commonplace in Jewish communities and academia to deny that "Judeo-Christian" has any real referent—it is argued that "Judeo-Christian" simply and always reduces to "Christian." Azoulay proposes that one of the most central projects of modern Western colonialism is precisely to *create* the "Judeo-Christian," not least through the violent redistribution of ancient Jewish communities to nearly two countries alone (the United States and the State of Israel, followed distantly by France, Canada, and the United Kingdom). Because the "Judeo-Christian" cannot exist without negating the Islamic, and because it seeks to claim Jews for the Christian side of the divide it both imagines and enforces, "Muslim Jews" becomes an act of reclamation and resistance against colonial domination.

The structure of Azoulay's book suggests this radical conclusion is meant to emerge more or less naturally from reflection on the family histories overwritten by Zionism. Whether others would be led to a similar conclusion through their own such exercises is less clear. Mizrahim in Israel are disproportionately right-wing. Shlaim and Hayoun follow Azoulay in repudiating "Mizrahi," but their stories share important similarities with those told by counterparts on the center and right, such as the Iraqi-Jewish journalist Lyn Julius in *Uprooted: How 3000 Years of Jewish Civilisation in the Arab World Vanished Overnight* (2018). Following these divergences is essential to understanding the complex position of these Jews vis-à-vis the State of Israel, Palestinians, and the "West."



---

## II. The Left Hand and the Right

**Best known today** as one of the Israeli "New Historians" (alongside others such as Ilan Pappé and Benny Morris), Shlaim was born in Baghdad in 1945, a period when Iraq had achieved formal sovereignty as the "Hashemite Kingdom of Iraq" but remained subordinate to the British Empire under the terms of the Anglo-Iraqi Treaty of 1930. Briefly overthrown by pro-Nazi Iraqi military officers in April 1941, the British defeated the coup by May and re-asserted their authority.

Perhaps because the short-lived independent regime was so virulently antisemitic, many Iraqis saw the return of British imperialism as a conspiracy of Jewish interests, and the worst incident of anti-Jewish mob violence in Iraqi history took place in June. In a two-day pogrom known as the Farhud, more than one hundred Jews were killed and hundreds more were injured; more than a thousand homes and businesses were damaged, with looting amounting to millions of pounds. This event is often linked in popular histories with the eventual mass emigration of Iraqi Jewry to Israel ten years later, though Zionist emissaries who visited the country in the mid-1940s complained that it seemed to have already passed from consciousness, and Shlaim's childhood memories as related in *Three Worlds* seem scarcely colored by it at all.

The three worlds of his title are those of his youth: Iraq, Israel, and England. The first occupies half of the book, though Shlaim left Baghdad when he was five years old. This is partly because Shlaim cannot resist the historian's instincts to contextualize his family's experience within the imperial and colonial history of Iraq, and partly because of the emotional tenor of the book. After emigrating to Israel, Shlaim writes, his grandmothers continued to view Iraq "as the beloved homeland while the Land of Israel was a place of exile. Their true feeling could have been expressed by a reversal of Psalm 137: 'By the waters of Zion, there we sat down, and there we wept, when we remembered Babylon.'" Of course, as he also tells us, his family had been very wealthy in Iraq, with a palatial home and servants, while in Israel they struggled to remain in the lower middle class. His parents, Yusef Shlaim and Saida Obadiah, were also Baghdad-born; they had "extended families, many friends, a support network, and a high social status. Before the birth of Israel and the first Arab-Israeli war, the thought of leaving the country for good would have been inconceivable."



**Because the "Judeo-Christian" negates the Islamic, and because it claims Jews for the Christian side of the divide it both imagines and enforces, "Muslim Jews" becomes for Azoulay an act of resistance.**

The Iraqi-Jewish community was the wealthiest among Middle Eastern Jewry, though most Iraqi Jews were not as well-off as Shlaim's family, and a variety of political orientations flourished. As in interwar Eastern Europe, Communists, socialists, and Zionists all vied with patriotic Iraqi liberals and nationalists for the hearts and minds of the Jewish community. Nevertheless, Shlaim relates that when he later asked his parents whether they had any Zionist friends, Obadiah invoked ethnicity rather than class: "No! Zionism is an Ashkenazi thing. It had nothing to do with us!"

Despite these attitudes, the defeat of the Arab armies by the State of Israel in 1948, followed by a series of bombings of Baghdad Jewish institutions between April 1950 and June 1951, marked a turning point for Iraqi Jews, culminating in their departure *en masse* for Israel. Something like the American hostility toward Muslims after 9/11, or toward the Japanese during World War II, took hold: every Jew was assumed to be a Zionist and possibly a spy for Israel, regardless of how loudly they proclaimed their liberalism, communism, or Iraqi nationalism. Even non-Zionist or anti-Zionist Jews could be alarmed by the "blood-curdling rhetoric about throwing the Jews into the sea," Shlaim writes, or could take satisfaction in the defeat of the overconfident armies of the Arab states, especially if the Palestinian experience of the war—the destruction and expulsion of the Nakba—was left out of consideration.

The bombings, which killed three or four Jews and injured others, helped convert these feelings into the more radical choice to leave the country of one's ancestors forever. In this regard, Shlaim's book contains a piece of sensationalist interest: he claims to settle seventy-five years of controversy over the alleged perpetrators. From the moment Iraqi Jews arrived in Israel, some claimed that Zionists had been responsible, all too eager to provoke immigration to Israel. In March 1950, when the Iraqi government first enacted a denaturalization law offering Jews the chance to leave for Israel by renouncing their Iraqi citizenship, very few took up the offer. The bombings, which began a month later, greatly exacerbated the sense that Iraq was no longer a safe home for Jews, and over the ensuing months emigration accelerated a thousandfold. Israeli authorities long denied any involvement, blaming the Iraqi right-wing nationalist party al-Istiqlal; after all, the reasoning went, the Iraqi government would also benefit from Jewish emigration as long as migrants were forced to forfeit their property at the border. Shlaim splits the difference, claiming that "three of the five bombs were the work of the Zionist underground in Baghdad."

His argument rests on the work of Yaacov Karkoukli, an Israeli born in Baghdad in 1928, who claimed in interviews with Shlaim to have been part of a Zionist activist circle that included members who carried out the attacks. Karkoukli justifies the terror as a means of accelerating Jewish emigration but stresses that the attacks were not directed by the Israeli state and that meticulous preparation was made to minimize loss of life. Shlaim treats Karkoukli's claims as mostly but not wholly reliable given their consistency with the Lavon Affair of 1954, which led to the resignation of Israeli defense minister Pinhas Lavon following public confessions by Egyptian Jews whom Israeli intelligence had recruited to plant bombs in U.S. Information Services offices in Cairo and Alexandria as part of a false flag operation meant to sow division between Egypt and the West. (Lavon always denied having given the order, and it was not until 2005 that the State of Israel acknowledged the operation when it honored nine Egyptian Jews who had been involved.) What clinches the case for Shlaim is an extract from a Baghdad police report in Karkoukli's possession—"undeniable proof," he writes, "of Zionist involvement in the terrorist attacks that helped to terminate two and a half millennia of Jewish presence in Babylon."

I am not the scholar to confirm or refute Shlaim's claims. In 1942 David Ben-Gurion had said that "if there are diasporas that it is our obligation to eliminate with the greatest possible urgency by bringing those Jews to the homeland, it is the Arab diasporas. . . . If we do not eliminate the Iraq exile by Zionist means, there is a danger that it will be eliminated by Hitlerite means." This much is clear: with the mass exodus of 120,000 Iraqi Jews by the end of 1951, many of whom were airlifted directly by Israel, both Ben-Gurion and al-Istiqlal got their wish.

What happened upon arrival in Israel forms the basis of the "Mizrahi" narrative largely shared by left and right. In Shlaim's accounting, Iraqi Jews were soon joined by 45,000 Jews from Yemen, 31,000 from Turkey, 21,000 from Iran, 16,000 from Egypt, 30,000 from Morocco, 13,000 from Tunisia, 31,000 from Libya, and 1,500 from Algeria. (The low number from Algeria is significant; Algerian Jews mostly remained there until independence in 1962, and then emigrated to France rather than Israel.) All these refugees, whom Israeli officials called *olim* ("immigrants"), were met with second-class citizenship and experiences of degradation that continue to shape Israeli politics and culture. Some were sprayed with the pesticide DDT upon their arrival at the airport, as if their countries of origin were inherently dirty. (This story has been immortalized by the Iraqi-Jewish author Sami Michael in his 1974 novel, *All Men Are Equal—But Some Are More*.) They were then sent to the *ma'abarot*, transit camps where they lived in tents or corrugated iron shacks, with limited water and almost no employment opportunities. Some of these camps were surrounded by barbed wire and guarded by police, viewed as potential breeding grounds for crime.

Education, which could have served as a route out of this situation, largely failed to fulfill this promise for Mizrahi children. Instead it ham-handedly tried to shoehorn them into the Zionist narrative of European-as-Jewish history, informed by foreign minister Abba Eban's worry that "the goal must be to instill in them a Western spirit, and not let them drag us into an unnatural orient." (It is not hard to multiply such quotations. The Polish-born Yitzhak Gruenbaum, first interior minister of Israel, said in 1943 that "We, the Jews, are twentieth-century people of Europe, whereas the Arab population is still at the developmental level of the fifteenth and sixteenth centuries. . . . the Mandate government must conduct its affairs based on the point of view that Palestine is a European country like England or its dominions." Records of Zionist emissaries to Arab Jewish communities prior to the establishment of the state are full of disparaging comments on the quality of the "human material.") Shlaim testifies to this condescending posture: one German-Jewish teacher of his "made some disparaging remarks about Orientals and their decadent habit of wearing jewelry. Then she turned to me and ordered me to remove my necklace and ring." In the face of this contempt, it was his parents' decision to send him to England for school that made it possible for Shlaim to become the scholar and public intellectual now known around the globe for his critical analysis of Zionism and his eloquent criticism of the Israeli government. (Pappé and Morris, like the other Israeli New Historians, are of European descent.)



Two decades of humiliations of this nature culminated with the Mizrahim taking revenge on the Ashkenazi elite by voting in Menachem Begin and the Likud in 1977, ending the thirty-year reign of the Labor Party. It was perhaps not inevitable that this revolt should have taken a "right-wing" form. The Israeli Black Panthers, founded in 1971, sought to combine demands for ethnic/racial justice with a broader left-wing program, similar to its American namesake. But Begin—himself Ashkenazi, like most subsequent Likud leadership, including Benjamin Netanyahu—wound up reaping the benefits of increased Mizrahi political consciousness through canny appeals to this slighted and snubbed community. In Shlaim's words, "he related to them at the emotional level as proud, patriotic, equal fellow citizens. . . . Begin gave all of us a voice, and united all of us against the Ashkenazi-Mapai establishment, regardless of our country of origin in the Muslim world."

The left and right have competing explanations for Likud's reliable base of Mizrahi support. The right contends that the Mizrahim "know the Arabs," carrying from their homelands a long legacy of oppression and mistrust that naturally inclines them toward more hawkish policies. The left asserts that "hatred of the Arabs was deliberately cultivated in Israel by unprincipled politicians in order to gain power and prolong their hold on it," as Shlaim puts it. On this account, the psychological wages of anti-Arab and anti-Palestinian sentiment are clear: the more the Ashkenazi establishment likens you to Arabs and portrays you as a threat, the more you respond by out-flanking them in your patriotism, nationalism, and anti-Arabism.

Shlaim does not narrate his way out of his own youthful attraction to this type of politics. Instead, *Three Worlds* ends with his IDF service in the mid-'60s, when he still "veered to the right of the political spectrum and shared the militant nationalism that was its hallmark," with his eventual move to the left only coming "many years later." The essence of that turn was his coming to believe that "the Zionist movement and the State of Israel have actively worked to erase our common past, our intertwined histories and our centuries-old heritage of pluralism, religious tolerance, cosmopolitanism and co-existence." The solution he envisions here is "remembering the past," which teaches that "there is nothing inevitable or pre-ordained about Jewish-Arab antagonism." His latest book, *Genocide in Gaza* (2025), takes a stand against the most recent and most monstrous outcome of that narrative.



As an elder, Shlaim is able to draw on his own hazy memories of childhood in Baghdad. But his attitude is mirrored by Hayoun, a millennial born in Los Angeles, when he writes in *When We Were Arabs* of the need to "paint for you a lost world to prove that we existed." The title has the quality of paradox: Is it really possible that the grandparents who raised him, Daida (Tunisian) and Oscar (Moroccan-Egyptian), "were" Jewish Arabs, while he "is" not? Hayoun moves one step past remembering, rejecting the notion that to be an Egyptian or Tunisian Jew is to be "forever part of a bygone era of romance and poetry." To do this, Hayoun intends his book "to breathe life into my grandparents and to avenge their lives, which multiple incarnations of imperialist white supremacy truncated and warped to political ends." He laments the degree to which Oscar and Daida succumbed to generations of French, British, and Israeli pressure "to view themselves as something—anything—other than Arab."

As an American and a millennial, Hayoun is self-conscious about this identity: he understands it as something that he is *claiming*, not a biological or ontological truth but a move in a political war of position. His grandparents found the prospect provocative—asked once "if we were Arabs," Daida reacted as if the word were a slur: "You sound like the Askenaz." Prodded to clarify, she responded that she was Tunisian. Oscar joined in, asking bemusedly: "Yes, what else are we [if not Arabs]?" Hayoun sees not only Jews but also Muslims and Christians as having "drunk the colonial Kool-Aid" with respect to contempt for Arab identity. Like many marginalized writers seeking to reclaim and valorize what has been disparaged, Hayoun walks a tightrope between wanting to "recall the beauty of a degraded people" and "promoting something akin to a Make America Great Again mentality." How, he asks, "does one champion an ethnic identity without falling into the pit of tribal nationalism?"



**We usually understand "divide and rule" as a tactic for dividing populations. But it also divides people from their own pasts.**

Hayoun travels to his grandparents' homelands but finds no easy answer. A visit to Egypt reveals little that resembles the bygone world depicted in the Golden Age cinema of his grandparents' generation: the dapper, cosmopolitan men and women combining the best of the European and Middle Eastern worlds. Hayoun feels the truth of Thomas Wolfe's observation that "you can't go home again." Yet on a visit to Casablanca, he reports that "the very cells in my body seemed to recognize the air there." On a trip to Tunisia for the first time with his mother Nadia, in the months after Daida's death, the cab driver taking them to Daida's old street, upon learning that his passengers were Jewish Tunisians, offered a welcome home and "a stick of *adamhot*, Tunisian fish eggs in a waxy cylinder, a traditional treat thought to originate in the Jewish community."

Going home again, literally and metaphorically, is central to all these narratives. So it is, of course, to narratives of the Nakba and of Palestinian refugees, with which stories of the Jews of Arab countries have increasingly been linked over the past several decades. The comparison goes straight to the heart of Azoulay's book. Her account is worth quoting at length:

> For a long time, I refrained from comparing the expulsion of the Jews from Algeria and the expulsion of Palestinians from Palestine. The Zionist instrumentalization of such symmetry as the basis for rejecting Palestinians' demands makes it very difficult to find a way to articulate this. To a certain extent, however, such a comparison can be generative, for it forces one to ask how the expulsion of the Jews, facilitated by their conversion into Europeans and Euro-Zionists,

became the exchange rate of decolonization. That is: How did it become acceptable for Jewish bodies to be trafficked between (French) Christians and (Algerian) Muslims? And how did this traffic imposed through international agreements of decolonization contribute to the possible (non-) solutions offered to Palestinians—especially in a world where assimilation aligned all Jews with the Euro-American Christian world?



---



## III. THE HAND OF NAPOLEON AND THE HAND OF GOD

**THE QUESTION** of returning home, of "bygone" eras and "vanished" worlds, is the thread running through all the letters in *The Jewelers of the Ummah*. A half-century ago, Memmi already wrote in *Juifs et Arabes* (1974) that "it is far too late to become Jewish Arabs again." Azoulay, born in what she makes a point of calling the "Zionist colony in Palestine" in the year of Algerian independence as a Muslim nation-state, reminds us that this very sense of belatedness is among the sensibilities that colonialism strives to produce.

We usually understand "divide and rule" as a tactic for dividing populations, preventing them from unifying to overthrow the colonial power. But "divide and rule" also divides people from their own pasts. Not only is the period before the arrival of the colonizer portrayed as primitive, but the colonizing power positions itself as arbiter of what is great in the cultural heritage of the colonized, declaring the living cultures to be "degenerate" versions of some preferred past. Thus history itself, like the land, becomes the property of the colonizer, and the colonized come to understand themselves as belated, living in the wake of some long-ago Golden Age.

Much of Azoulay's book concerns the way the French made this move in Algeria, with particular reference to architecture and craft. From the moment they arrived in 1830, the French made catalogues of Algerian art. They took photos, made drawings, and seized individual pieces to display in French museums. They bulldozed entire neighborhoods full of craft shops, drove craftspeople out of business, and recruited young Algerian girls to schools where they taught them how to weave their own styles in a "modern" way.

The effect, Azoulay perceptively demonstrates, was quite literally to disembody. In her own photos of Algerian-Jewish jewelry, bracelets and necklaces are always hanging on human beings, on their arms and necks and torsos; in the French catalogues they hover in the air against a white background, numbered for ease of reference. These colonial inventories "sought to make sure that both unruly people and unruly objects were under control," Azoulay writes. The scholars who compiled them imagined that they could isolate the "pure" form of each piece, capturing what was essential so that French jewelers could replicate the art, ideally using machinery for mass production. But this colonial dream was always impossible. By wrenching these objects from the hands of their creators and their social world, colonialism sought to transform those objects and that world into something else entirely.

In *Discourse on Colonialism* (1950), Aimé Césaire developed the notion of the imperial boomerang: the repression that colonial powers perpetrate abroad ultimately gets unleashed at home. *Jewelers of the Ummah* identifies something like the reverse phenomenon within European history: the creation of internal colonies at home preparing the dominating power to erect external colonies abroad. Before the French did this to the Algerians, that is, they did it to themselves—to French Jews, and even to French Christians. Just four decades before the colonization of Algeria, in a frenzy of anti-religious sentiment, French revolutionaries of the First Republic suppressed the Catholic Church, nationalized its property, and abolished the Gregorian calendar (instituted by Pope Gregory XIII in 1582), purging its names and holidays of old gods and reorienting time itself—away from the Christian liturgy, toward the atheism of the Cult of Reason and the rationalist deism of the Cult of the Supreme Being.

Emperor Napoleon Bonaparte in turn abolished the Republican calendar in 1805, even though it was "too late" for him to ever be King of France. "It was by making myself a Catholic that I won the war in the Vendée," he had said, "by making myself a Moslem that I established myself in Egypt, by making myself an ultramontane that I turned men's hearts toward me in Italy. If I were to govern a nation of Jews I would rebuild the Temple of Solomon." It is a striking token of imperial prerogative that Napoleon, a born and baptized Catholic, could speak of "making himself a Catholic" (and even an ultramontane, a papist *par excellence*), notwithstanding his excommunication in retaliation for his annexation of the Papal States.

Whatever this man was, he subjugated Catholics, Protestants, Muslims, and Jews. Like conquerors throughout history, he called this subjugation "emancipation," and everywhere there were those who were drawn to this promise and those who saw through it. Azoulay mentions the Egyptian campaign, famously documented by the historian and scholar Abd al-Rahman al-Jabarti. Faced with a conqueror who proclaimed allegiance to *liberté*, *egalité*, and *fraternité*, al-Jabarti responded by rejecting those things. Nor was he swayed by Napoleon's boast that he had defeated Islam's old enemy, the Pope. As al-Jabarti saw it, that only meant that Napoleon was not a Christian at all but some new thing—a traitor to all religions, including Christendom.

Al-Jabarti's suspicions were mirrored in European regions that Napoleon conquered, within their own local contexts. Thanks to Napoleon's export of the principles of the Revolution, religious minorities in the conquered territories—Protestants in Catholic-majority areas, Catholics in Protestant ones, as well as Jews everywhere—were "emancipated" in the sense that they could pursue higher education and enter professions previously closed to them. But after Napoleon's defeat in 1815, these changes were rolled back and permanently identified with the hated French. Religious qualifications were reintroduced, and reaction was the order of the day. The counterrevolutionaries of Prussia, Bavaria, and the Papal States would have understood al-Jabarti perfectly.

This was never a simple story of checkered progress, of two steps forward and one step back. The "emancipators," including such luminaries as the Abbé Grégoire in France and Christian Wilhelm von Dohm in Prussia, understood individual Jewish rights as contingent upon collective Jewish disappearance. Emancipation was tied to "regeneration" and "civic improvement," upon the Jews' becoming useful, loyal lovers of the state, as indistinguishable from Christians as possible in their appearance, speech, demeanor, and customs. These were the explicit terms of the deal, and it did not take twentieth-century postcolonial theory to see it. Supposedly isolated, "uneducated" Jewish communities in the Russian empire grasped the stakes perfectly well. Hasidic masters lined up on both sides of the question, some seeing Napoleon as a potential liberator from tsarist oppression and agent of messianic return to the land of Israel, while others—most notably the Alter Rebbe, founder of Chabad Hasidism—saw him as a rebel against God.

Ultimately, the French made this same offer to Algerian Jews, though only after subjecting them to the same colonial violence and dispossession as Algerian Muslims. Azoulay is emphatic on this last point, intensely preoccupied with debunking the myth that Algerian Jews jumped at the opportunity to ally themselves with the colonizers. Drawing on work by scholars like Joshua Schreier and Sarah Abrevaya Stein, as well as her own research, she describes four decades of failed struggle on the part of the French to win voluntary allegiance, culminating with the imposition of citizenship by force with the Crémieux Decree of 1870, which granted citizenship to most Algerian Jews (excluding southern, Saharan Jews) during the Franco-Prussian War. Jews from France who had already taken Napoleon's deal played a key role in this struggle, founding the Alliance Israélite Universelle (AIU) in 1860. Their aim, as an AIU circular from 1896 put it, was to "send a ray of light from Western culture to the communities that have become ossified in the course of hundreds of years of repression and backwardness." The AIU pursued this *mission civilisatrice* through education, promoting French language and culture primarily to Algerian Jewish children. Azoulay calls these AIU teachers, along with the rabbis sent from the Central Consistory of France to supplant the local religious authorities, "converts to a new form of being-a-Jew."

Another of her central arguments is that the Algeria created by anticolonial struggle converted its people to a parallel new form of being-a-Muslim, a nation-state form dispossessed of its Jewish past. In other words, the new Algerian government collaborated with the French in defining Algeria as Muslim and Jews as European; indeed it achieved independence in part by sacrificing its Jews. Suspicion had intensified during the revolution, Jews being perceived as aligned with the French given the grant of citizenship; by 1957 the FLN had shifted away from its earlier position that Jews were integral to Algeria and began attacking Jewish institutions. In this way, Azoulay suggests, all the Arab governments that cast suspicion on their Jewish populations in the wake of the birth of the State of Israel were and remain complicit with Zionism and the longer-term colonial project of Europe. The point has occasionally been recognized in the halls of Arab power, and not just by the PLO; in 1975 the government of Iraq invited all Iraqi Jews to return, promising full citizenship rights. But to repeat Memmi's words from that same year, it was by then perceived as "too late."

Azoulay seizes on moments from her family history that highlight resistance to colonial domination. Her grandfather Joseph deserted the French army during World War I; her great-grandmother Marianne decided in 1895 to name her daughter Aïcha (as if to say, in one of Azoulay's many memorable chapter titles, "Fuck you, France, my daughter is Islam"), even if that daughter grew up to name her own son—Azoulay's father—Roger Lucien. *Jewelers* thus weaves together broad colonial dynamics with intimate, familiar ones, both brutal and delicate.

**Nationalization, like racialization, is always ongoing. It is never only, or merely, a *fait accompli*. And it is because it is continually taking place that it can be resisted.**

Craft is the knot that ties these threads together. For Azoulay, craft represents embeddedness, the complete life that colonizers cut apart by separating "religion" from "ethnicity" from "citizenship" from "economic activity" from "language" from "culture" and on and on. Her picture is of a prelapsarian harmony undone by decade after decade of domination. As "the jewelers of the ummah," Algerian Jews were at one with their life-world, in the manner of all *indigènes*. Colonial divide-and-rule worked relentlessly over 130 years to shatter it—not only to erase it but to erase the erasure, destroying the very memory of Jews as African, Algerian, and indigenous. The products of this process were either individuals of "Jewish" faith, fit to be citizens of Western liberal countries, or "Jews," members of a national entity fit to colonize Palestine. Azoulay's central purpose is to reject this dichotomy.

This brings us full circle, back to the challenge she poses to the "progressive" left. Craft has often been portrayed as the very paradigm of romantic nostalgia—the first victim of technological supersessionism—while Luddism is widely seen as the epitome of the lost cause. On this, liberal capitalist progressivism and "orthodox" Marxism have always agreed. Next to their scientific and technological realism, the idealism of the great champion of craft, the English socialist William Morris, has always been derided as fuzzy. "People interested . . . in the details of the arts of life feel a desire to revert to methods of handicraft for production in general," Morris wrote in 1888. "It may therefore be worth considering how far this is a mere reactionary sentiment incapable of realization, and how far it may foreshadow a real coming change in our habits of life." This is Azoulay's problem as well: the possibility of reviving and restoring a murdered culture.





For her, resistance to something as massive and insidious as the "too late" of colonial temporality, the imposed running-forward of historical time, begins with personal practice. She stops thinking of herself as Israeli, as Mizrahi, and instead thinks of herself as a Palestinian and Algerian Jew. She teaches her hands to make the motions her ancestors made, to create jewelry. And of course, she speaks and writes to the dead, hoping through conversation with Marianne, Roger, and her mother Zahava as well as with Hannah Arendt, Frantz Fanon, and Ghassan Kanafani to come to an understanding with the past. All this is based on the premise that since the colonial project continues in the present, it continues precisely in us. Nationalization, like racialization, is always ongoing. It is never only, or merely, a *fait accompli*. And it is because it is continually taking place that it can be resisted, in ways that may not require imagining a utopian turning back of the clock or undoing of what has been done. Azoulay knows the possibility will strike many as even more remote, even more belated, amid the destruction of Gaza; she completed the manuscript before the violence had erupted. Still she believes that "Palestine can still be the site of the ultimate collapse of this crusade."

In the swamp of social media, the word "RETVRN," with its substitution of an ancient Roman "V" for "U," is now used to mock—viciously or playfully, depending on context—a certain type of reactionary obsessed with classical aesthetics and eager to roll back modernity. For readers whose primary understanding of the left is "progressive," Azoulay's approach to decolonization may seem uncomfortably close to this sensibility. "We must *return* to what colonialism has deprived us of," she writes. At the end of the book, she imagines the granddaughter of a character in Kanafani's 1969 novella *Returning to Haifa* resisting what domination has wrought by reclaiming the name of her Arab ancestors:

> The return has already started. Here I am . . . breaking the Zionist spell over my body, over the land, over our prophetic powers. These are powers that can assist us in healing, in immersing ourselves in the seven years of repair the Torah calls for, renewing our gratitude to our life among others, respecting the balance and secrets of the world and living under their mantle.



I would invite readers inclined to dismiss all this as flagrant or feeble romanticism to consider that the distance between Morris and Marx has been overstated. Marx, after all, wrote in *Capital* that in "manufacture and handicrafts, the workman makes use of a tool, in the factory, the machine makes use of him." His grandfather was a rabbi; his father, who began practicing law after being "emancipated" by Napoleon, had to enter the Christian Evangelical church of Prussia to maintain his career after Napoleon's defeat. Little wonder he was able to perceive liberalism as an ambiguous form of "progress," and after all the set of people moved by the *Communist Manifesto*'s critique of capitalism for destroying what we cherish—"all that is solid melts into air, all that is holy is profaned"—has long included conservatives.

For myself, I do not need Marx's authority to license Azoulay's potential history of the Jewish Muslim world, or Shlaim and Hayoun's rejection of Memmi's claim that it is "too late to be Arab Jews." I think instead of the way the rabbinic sages of Palestine and Babylonia grappled with the question of resurrection in the wake of their own destruction and loss, not just of the Temple but the entire way of life associated with ancient Judaism. They began with the simple acknowledgment of the Jewish daily liturgy that resurrection is God's business: *Blessed are You, YHVH our God, who makes the dead live*. In their clever and wise way, however, they went on to identify other times in life when this phrase should be recited. Upon waking up in the morning, they said, one should thank God for resurrection. A day of rain, when the land is nourished, is akin to resurrection. Seeing a friend one has not seen for a year, one thanks God for resurrection.

In sanctifying these mundanities with the dignity of the most extreme miracle, the rabbis tell us that we should not be so haughty with our assumptions about what is possible, or where the line lies between human power and the divine. In the everyday, practical work of our hands, the world where the highest value is to "see the light" may vanish. **BR**

Image: Getty Images

# THE REAL PATH TO ABUNDANCE

*Sandeep Vaheesan*

*Abundance*
Ezra Klein and Derek Thompson
Avid Reader Press, $30

**IN THEIR NEW BOOK,** *Abundance*, Ezra Klein and Derek Thompson argue that American liberals have ironically succumbed to a conservative worldview, in the original sense of "conservative."

After a midcentury boom, their story goes, progressives became skeptical of growth. To keep development from running roughshod over marginalized communities and the environment, liberals created a thicket of rules and regulations meant to constrain business power as well as the government itself. But these "anti-growth" policies are now causing harm in their own right, while China has been demonstrating just how much a nation can do when it is *not* so constrained. Though Joe Biden's investments in renewables, chips, and infrastructure were a step in the right direction, Klein and Thompson say, too much red tape and too little ambition are still preventing the development of clean energy, plentiful housing, and life-saving drugs for all. Instead of delivering progress, liberals are enforcing scarcity, hamstringing government, and smothering innovation—all in the name of progressive values.



As a foil, the book opens with a utopian vision of the United States in 2050—a world where government has gotten out of its own way and learned to build things again, or at least allowed them to be built. For Klein and Thompson, this includes drones that deliver anti-aging pills right to your doorstep and AI that reduces the work week for "most people." Looking back from that imagined future, an unnamed narrator laments:

> For years, we accepted homelessness and poverty and untreated disease and declining life expectancy. For years, we knew what we needed to build to alleviate the scarcities so many faced and create the opportunities so many wanted, and we simply didn't build it. For years, we failed to invent and implement technology that would make the world cleaner, healthier, and richer. For years, we constrained our ability to solve the most important problems.

Klein and Thompson thus set out to defend what they call "a simple idea: to have the future we want, we need to build and invent more of what we need." They want a "liberalism that builds."

Who wouldn't agree with that? This rhetoric, like much of the writing throughout the book, isn't just "simple." It constantly verges on platitude or tautology, concealing consequential political, economic, and moral judgments behind a veneer of common sense. And it does so in language that repeatedly echoes the entrepreneurial mantras of the world's most powerful corporations. We have to move faster, Klein and Thompson say. Stop worrying so much about breaking things, they imply. But "politics is not just about the problems we have," as the authors rightly observe. "It's about the problems we see." Unfortunately, *Abundance* itself suffers from a severe case of myopia.

There are many causes of "untreated disease," for example. Most salient to the authors are the not-yet-invented miracle drugs that would make pharmaceutical companies a fortune. But the book says little about most other causes—not even to weigh their relative contribution to our medical scarcity. Perhaps most notably, Klein and Thompson entirely ignore the intellectual property regime that protects pharmaceutical companies' extraordinary wealth and power at the expense of citizens' health by granting decades of patent monopoly frequently in exchange for nominal benefits to patients. Is a nation that leaves all this intact with the hope of plentiful daily medication really "the future we want"? Klein and Thompson might support patent reform too, but they never train their attention on *that* problem. Instead, with laser-like focus, *Abundance* again and again blames a real and urgent issue—poverty, homelessness, dirty energy, disease—on a simple and familiar villain: well-meaning but short-sighted liberals who are more concerned with tying things up than getting things done.

Like any good story, there are grains of truth in this one. Many readers will find it persuasive, primed by decades of anti-government rhetoric directed at certain state activities from Democrats and Republicans alike. But the reality is that the authors' concrete agenda, so far as it is discernible in this mostly rhetorical book, is much more likely to perpetuate the ugliest aspects of the United States today than to deliver utopia for everyone.

That does not mean that abundance, or better-functioning government, is not a desirable end: it is. But achieving it requires breaking with the ethos of neoliberalism—its deference to private capital and hostility to public governance—that structures so much of Klein and Thompson's thinking, even when they are praising Biden's "post-neoliberal" industrial policy. A much more promising path to abundance than the one this book offers is to embrace a twenty-first-century New Deal. That is the tried-and-true model for a "liberalism that builds" in the United States, and *Abundance* rightly invokes it as a foil to the present. Yet Klein and Thompson strangely shy away from calling for a new (or Green) New

Deal. And they display little understanding of how the old one actually worked, both in terms of politics and in terms of policy.

---

**TO BE SURE,** Klein and Thompson are not hostile to government in the same way that hard-line free market fundamentalists are. They do not view government as inherently inefficient, nor do they wish to drown it in the bathtub. "The right lesson from World War II and Warp Speed"—the public-private partnership launched during Trump's first administration to spearhead COVID-19 vaccines—"is that the state is no enemy of invention or innovation," they write. "In fact, the government can accelerate both." They clearly think government has a central role to play in delivering abundance.





**Politics is "about the problems we see," Klein and Thompson rightly observe. Unfortunately, *Abundance* suffers from a severe case of myopia.**

Still, the role they see for it is mostly limited to fiscal support for the private sector, and their main target is what they consider excessive government bureaucracy. Throughout the book, the authors direct their ire at local zoning rules that bar the construction of multifamily housing, condition development on minimum parking requirements, or otherwise outlaw dense residential construction. And they repeatedly criticize environmental review processes that they claim delay, inhibit, or render construction of clean energy and transmission infrastructure prohibitively expensive. Remove these hurdles, *Abundance* contends, and private actors will deliver abundance—at least when goaded by sufficiently high levels of public subsidy.

The authors back these claims with anecdotes of regulations and bureaucrats supposedly stifling development. This is not rigorous argument, however, but a "story," as the authors themselves put it on the last page of the book. The problem is that stories can be deeply misleading. Where this one doesn't give a mistaken impression through sins of omission, it simply gets things wrong. It often blames government for bad outcomes where it should be blaming the whole structure of the market—including other government policies (among them too *little* regulation of the private sector) and, especially, the nature of private investment (even when spurred by government subsidy).

Take housing construction, a notoriously volatile industry. Many American cities are indeed facing an affordable housing crisis. Over the last half-century, U.S. housing starts—the number of privately owned units being constructed—reached a peak in 2006 before cratering in the run-up to the global financial crisis of 2008; they have not recovered since. Klein and Thompson acknowledge as much. But they fail to note that zoning rules can't possibly be the primary driver of this stagnation.

In fact, one of the central themes of *Abundance*—dynamic Texas versus sclerotic California—ironically undercuts the myopic focus on zoning. Klein and Thompson note that states like Texas today are building more housing than liberal strongholds like California, which they view as the epitome of blue state misgovernance. But the Golden State built plenty of housing in the mid-aughts. In fact, at times in 2004 and 2005, California even permitted more new housing units than Texas did. Since zoning restrictions didn't suddenly get tighter in the second half of the 2000s, this building boom scrambles the thesis that public land-use controls are the root cause of today's housing crisis. The authors fail to note the many determinants of housing starts, ignoring recent national dampers on homebuilding (including high interest rates and shortages of building materials and construction workers) as well as local factors such as much higher land prices and wages and the relative scarcity of undeveloped land in blue center cities in blue states.

But even if zoning and other onerous regulations aren't the primary reason for stagnant homebuilding, couldn't upzoning help? However intuitive the idea may seem, the evidence is mixed—nowhere near as strong as Klein and Thompson insinuate. Such reforms have already been pursued in many localities. A leading meta-study published in 2023 found, on average, a 0.8 percent expansion of the local housing stock three to nine years after such changes, with significant variation. Zoning reforms produced a modest increase in housing stock in some places but not much elsewhere.

Recent work by economists Schuyler Louie, John A. Mondragon, and Johannes Wieland is even more skeptical. They find that unaffordable housing in coastal cities is not caused by excess regulation. Instead, it is driven by high demand and high and rising incomes. As they put it, "our findings challenge the consensus that relaxing regulatory constraints would substantially lower housing prices and meaningfully expand housing quantities." In a recent study mapping the "many problems" in housing markets, legal scholars Ganesh Sitaraman and Christopher Serkin also conclude that "focusing exclusively—or even primarily—on loosening or eliminating zoning rules is misguided."



Zoning is certainly too restrictive in many low-density suburbs throughout the country, but it is hardly the principal reason that housing is very expensive in high-density San Francisco and comparatively cheap in less dense Houston. The findings of Louie, Mondragon, and Wieland present another reason: San Francisco is simply a "superstar city" (in Klein and Thompson's own words), while Houston is not. The simple story of California bad, Texas good does not stand up to scrutiny, at least on housing. Once a broader lens is brought to bear and rent is measured in relation to income, Texas looks much less like a success story.

As for energy, *Abundance* rightly stresses the need for more investment in zero-carbon power generation and transmission lines. But here the story of public barriers to abundance is even weaker. During the Biden administration, solar projects on public lands completed the environmental review process, on average, in less than six months, and between 2010 and 2021, few transmission projects required a time- and labor-intensive environmental impact statement. The real problems have to do with the authority to site transmission lines (which mostly remains at the state and local level, rather than with the federal government) and the bad incentives that shape the behavior of private transmission owners. Private management of the grid thwarts construction of lines that threaten the profits of investor-owned utilities and prevents timely connection of new generation facilities. In Kings County, California, solar projects that completed environmental review in a few months were stuck in the interconnection queue for an average of more than two years.

The excess procedure story is even less applicable to nuclear power. Setting aside public opposition, Klein and Thompson charge that the struggle to expand nuclear power in the United States "is not a failure of the private market to responsibly bear risk but of the federal government to properly weigh risk." In reality, federal law has capped the legal liability of nuclear plant operators in the event of accidents since 1957. The problems of the nuclear power industry in the United States lie elsewhere. Its history is one of massive construction delays, cost overruns, and poor operational performance. While plant performance has greatly improved in recent years, frequent outages, high costs of operation, and the growth of cheaper alternatives have led to the closure of many nuclear plants. Rather than being "too cheap to meter," as some nuclear proponents predicted in the 1950s, nuclear power has often proved too expensive and unreliable to keep in service.



**With laser-like focus, *Abundance* again and again blames a real and urgent issue—poverty, homelessness, dirty energy, disease—on a simple and familiar villain.**

For a case in point, consider the newest nuclear generation facilities in the United States: units 3 and 4 at Georgia Power's Plant Vogtle on the Savannah River. These units came online in 2023 and 2024, respectively—seven years late and tens of billions of dollars over initial cost estimates. Both the federal and state governments eagerly supported the project, and environmental reviews were completed in 2008 and 2011. But the contractors on the project (including Westinghouse) faced persistent problems finding workers with specialized skills, as well as materials, to build the plant. The project developers overpromised and consistently failed to deliver.

Similar problems afflicted the V.C. Summer nuclear project near Columbia, South Carolina, which would have added two units at an existing plant. The construction program was such a disaster that the two owners, private SCE&G and public Santee Cooper, abandoned the project in 2017 while at the same time securing legislative approval for recovering project costs from South Carolina customers. The old utility regulation principle of ratepayers paying only for "used and useful" capital investments is too often honored more in the breach than in observance.

Industry insiders, for their part, flatly contradict Klein and Thompson's assertion that the federal government is to blame. "The problem isn't the commitment of governments; it is the performance of the industry," Gregory Jaczko, the former chairman of the Nuclear Regulatory Commission, said last year. "We could 'solve' all 'regulatory and permitting' issues for nuclear tomorrow and not one new plant would get ordered or built," Jigar Shah, a top official in Biden's Department of Energy, tweeted in February.





This is the blind spot running through all of *Abundance*'s anecdotes: the limits of the private sector. The primary conceit is that in many areas, the private sector is ready to invest—and to invest big—if politicians would only lift public barriers standing in their way. There is little evidence that is true. In reality, corporate executives and managers make investment decisions based on expected profits. Even when zoning restrictions are favorable, developers evaluate a range of investment options before committing to construction. They are looking not only for positive returns but for *higher* returns than alternative options. Homebuilders, in particular, will not build unless they have reason to think they can achieve sufficiently high profits—those that outperform land banking, speculation, or other forms of investment. The much-touted housing boom in Austin is a case in point: after a few years of above-average building activity led to modest rent reductions, residential developers reduced construction substantially. The burst of construction made only a small dent in the dramatic increase in rents since 2010.

The same is true when it comes to renewable energy. In his recent book *The Price Is Wrong*, Brett Christophers shows that insufficient expected profits are a principal barrier to investment in solar and wind projects. Developers and lenders alike are reluctant to pursue and finance such projects unless they will deliver substantial and stable profits and are more attractive than other investment choices.

In addition to neglecting the central role of profit expectations in investment decisions, Klein and Thompson have nothing to say about the short-term orientation of today's large shareholder-dominated corporations. In general, shareholders withdraw far more capital from businesses than they invest, and they often demand massive dividends and stock buybacks and acquisitions in lieu of capital expenditures, let alone higher wages for workers. Given that CEO compensation is often tied to their company's stock price, top executives have little incentive to defy shareholder demands for cash.

Along with the state-guided enterprises of China, Klein and Thompson's preferred corporate model is the AT&T of midcentury—a highly innovative enterprise credited with developing technologies like the laser, photovoltaic cell, and transistor. They attribute AT&T's long-term orientation and accomplishments to its status as a secure, government-protected monopoly. If that AT&T existed today, large shareholders would balk at risky, long-term investment in speculative engineering and scientific projects. Indeed, this is what happened when a durable monopoly of our era tried to replicate the AT&T success. In 2010 Google set up Google X for an elite group of employees to pursue long-term projects, but by 2015 Chief Financial Officer Ruth Porat imposed a more short-term, cautious orientation on the venture as part of a broader effort to reduce costs and disburse more cash to shareholders. In the words of economist William Lazonick, whereas AT&T represented the American corporation practicing "retain and reinvest," Google is closer to the prevailing norm of "downsize and distribute."

The government could do a lot to change corporate behavior—by banning stock buybacks, for example, or requiring firms to give workers and consumers board representation. Yet except for a passing mention of stronger labor laws in the book's introduction, Klein and Thompson say nothing about the public regulation of corporations. What about the risk of collusion and other unfair business practices? As federal and state lawsuits allege, software company RealPage has enabled landlords across the nation to collude and prioritize higher rents over occupancy, boosting collective profits while keeping more units empty. And where does sectoral regulation fit in the *Abundance* vision? Public agencies have closely regulated the electric power sector for more than a century and helped make affordable electricity universal in the United States. These questions are central to effective regulatory design, and thus to any real abundance program, but Klein and Thompson are silent about them.

*Abundance* thus makes a very weak case for the supposed benefits of relaxing public governance. But it also misrepresents deregulation's obvious costs and regulation's clear benefits. Klein and Thompson acknowledge that federal environmental laws have been enormously successful in cleaning up the air, water, and land of the United States. (An EPA study found that the Clean Air Act Amendments of 1990 produced public health and welfare benefits, including preventing hundreds of thousands deaths annually, that exceeded the costs of compliance by a factor of 30 to 1.) But they suggest zoning and environmental review have outlived their justification.

This narrative rests on an imagined past of unfettered discretion for property owners. "In the 1800s, no American city had zoning rules," Klein and Thompson write. But public control of land use is hardly a twentieth-century phenomenon; it is rooted in the centuries-old common law of nuisance. A fundamental tenet of property law is that landowners cannot exercise their dominion in a way that injures others. Understood in this light, zoning and environmental review are statutory descendants of nuisance law. The difference is that they replace a judicial and remedial approach to the problem with an administrative and preventative one.

That is exactly why Klein and Thompson should look less harshly on them. The authors compare court-centric governance in the United States unfavorably with administrative governance in other nations. "Decisions that are often made by bureaucracies in other countries are made by judges in our country," they observe. They are correct that administrative decision-making is generally superior to judicial supremacy, both on public accountability and expertise grounds. But the practical effect of abandoning administrative zoning and environmental review in the United States would be to cede even greater power to judges. In the words of Christopher Serkin, "the ad hoc character of piecemeal nuisance litigation creates risk and uncertainty and enormous costs to the entire system."

While zoning rules are unduly restrictive in many affluent suburbs, they are often far too weak elsewhere. Many poor people, especially poor people of color, live in proximity to polluting facilities like oil refineries and power plants and bear disproportionate harms of polluted air and water, including higher incidences of asthma, cancer, and premature death. The Mississippi River corridor in Louisiana illustrates this problem: lined with oil refineries and petrochemical plants, it is dubbed Cancer Alley for the facilities' adverse effects on residents' health. Stronger zoning rules that separated such activities from residential areas would yield significant public health benefits.

Klein and Thompson say nothing at all about such issues—they simply write these impacts out of the story. In a notable passage, they credit Congress for exempting some new chip fabrication plants from NEPA review. What they don't say is that these facilities are highly polluting, contaminating air and groundwater. They were once concentrated in Santa Clara County, helping to make it the county with the most Superfund sites in the nation. There are obvious benefits to studying social and environmental impacts in advance and designing and siting industrial facilities with an eye toward minimizing them. Any serious public policy discussion must contend with tradeoffs—but Klein and Thompson see nothing but costs.





---

**IN ALL THESE WAYS,** *Abundance* misrepresents the costs and benefits of regulation. But it also misrepresents the political obstacles to abundant housing and abundant clean energy.

For the most part, that is because the book has little concrete political vision at all. Klein and Thompson repeatedly say that "we" are all in this together, depicting Americans as a monolith. It's clear enough why they write this way: they hope to recruit people to the cause. But good missionary rhetoric makes for bad analysis.

The one notable exception to the book's false universalism is its unstinting criticism of liberal, upper middle-class professionals—especially lawyers. This class is essentially opposed to growth, Klein and Thompson contend: it insists on larding process on top of process to thwart development, whether in the name of historic preservation, environmental protection, or simply in order to protect home values. The authors stress that it's not "the mother working two jobs" but the affluent who show up at local planning meetings to express opposition to new construction. And they take progressive professionals to task for missing "the contribution that liberal governance"—again, they mean excessive zoning—"made to the rise of Trumpism."

The authors are right that liberal failures contributed to Trump's rise, though those failures have much more to do with repudiating New Deal politics than with opposition to zoning reform. (More on that in the next section.) But by focusing its ire on this group—to the exclusion of other political villains—*Abundance* occludes where the most important fault lines in American society lie. We could not be further from the story of Thomas Piketty's *Capital in the Twenty-First Century*, with its clear portrait of patrimonial capitalists and lavishly compensated executives thriving at the expense of everyone else—as it happens, the same story that Bernie Sanders and Alexandria Ocasio-Cortez are telling as they travel the nation on their "Fighting Oligarchy" tour, which has turned out tens of thousands of people in places like Tucson, Arizona.





**The picture painted here could not be further from the story of Thomas Piketty's *Capital in the Twenty-First Century*, with its clear portrait of capitalists and executives thriving at the expense of everyone else.**

It's not insignificant that Klein and Thompson's attacks echo the Trumpist agenda they disclaim. The affluent undoubtedly have more time and resources to spend advocating for their interests than the poor. But instead of calling for steeper progressive taxation and anti-monopoly policies that would rein in the power of the affluent, Klein and Thompson focus single-mindedly on red tape. Instead of calling for expanded state capacity to expedite environmental reviews (as they do for some government projects, like California's High-Speed Rail Authority), they suggest we should ditch environmental review entirely. And instead of making the case for strengthening and broadening democratic participation in land use policy, they imply we should simply jettison it altogether. They do not call for these things explicitly. But their simplistic morality tales invite these conclusions, and the authors do nothing to guard against them.

This vision is undemocratic in both form and function. Diminishing public power over land use decisions means greater private control, which in turn means more deference to the whims of the market and more discretion for corporate executives and financiers—in short, more oligarchy. That is exactly what Trump and Elon Musk are hoping to achieve by taking the chainsaw to federal agencies, and that is why, as

Republican pollster Patrick Ruffini puts it, they are "hitting the professional-managerial class—and hitting them hard." These points of overlap with Trump's agenda also matter politically. Whatever one thinks of the merits of their policy proposals, Klein and Thompson present no evidence that Democrats—including the liberal professionals they condemn—will be energized by their anti-bureaucracy platform in the face of Trump's destructive attacks on government. Perhaps the authors believe that steep partisan polarization, along with growing disgust at Trump, give Democrats a rare agenda-setting opportunity to declare war on the liberal PMC—an integral part of its base—without suffering at the ballot box. But if so, they do not argue the point.

The book echoes today's oligarchy in another way, too: its embrace of Silicon Valley's vision for America. Klein and Thompson gush about AI's potential and want the United States to play a leading role in directing its development. Similarly, their transportation future says more about self-driving electric vehicles than about mass public transit. This is not the utopianism of Edward Bellamy or the Knights of Labor, but the familiar futurism of tech oligarchs.

To achieve it, Klein and Thompson do call on government to support research and development in the private sector—implicitly acknowledging that the corporate and public interest are not always aligned, and that markets, as presently constituted, won't deliver abundance on their own. But they are wary of how many conditions are placed on this fiscal support. "One problem liberals are facing at every level where they govern is that they often add too many goals to a single project," they write. "When the government adds the right number of goals, standards, and rules, much can be accomplished. When it adds too many, the project can collapse under its own weight." This "everything-bagel liberalism" is inhibiting development by making it too hard or too expensive to follow through.

There are real tradeoffs here—the authors are right about that, though in a trivial way. Too many conditions on public financing can certainly be counterproductive. But this is little more than a tautology. Simply being told that excessive conditions are excessive doesn't answer any of the hard questions; the real issue is how best to advance the public good in any particular case. Rather than propose surgical excisions or offer guidance about how to balance different aims, Klein and Thompson cast doubt on a broad range of public demands, from prevailing wage laws to green design standards, child care requirements for chips factories, and mandates for special air filtration systems for apartments located near highways.

The authors do not go so far as to insist that any one of these conditions should generally be given up. But because the book fails to give reasons for ever attaching any of these conditions to an actual project, readers are left with the impression that we might as well dispense with all of them. Never mind that prevailing wage requirements have been a foundation of federal contracting policy for nearly a century and worked harmoniously with the developmentalism of the 1930s, '40s, and '50s. Or that building energy-inefficient structures in an age of accelerating climate change is penny wise and pound foolish for society. Or that clean indoor air should not be a luxury in a society as wealthy as the United States in 2025. The final example is revealing: the paeans to a bountiful future in *Abundance* conceal an unacknowledged validation of scarcity.

As a result of these omissions, Klein and Thompson fail to convey the risks of overcorrecting in the opposite direction: a *plain*-bagel liberalism that simply hands money over with very few or even no conditions at all. We don't have to look very far to get a sense of how such an agenda would play out. Since the early 2010s, Musk's various ventures have been lavished with federal and state support, including low-cost credit, loan guarantees, and a variety of government contracts. Tesla and SpaceX would hardly exist if the government had not opened its coffers to them, with few if any conditions. These handouts have made Musk the wealthiest man on the planet, deepening oligarchy while providing only modest public benefits. After decades of federal support, electric vehicles accounted for only 8 percent of the total car market in 2024, and Tesla has a market share of under 5 percent. In China, by contrast, electric vehicles represented 40 percent of sales last year. Meanwhile, Tesla's precise impact on carbon emissions remains disputed—one study found that its claimed reductions are overstated by up to 49 percent—and SpaceX has largely stepped into the shoes previously filled by NASA, privatizing a once public function.

This is not a new phenomenon. In the nineteenth century, Congress awarded more than 170 million acres of land in the West—land cleared of indigenous people through mass killing and evictions by the federal government—to rail companies to construct lines from the Midwest to the West Coast. The total land grant was nearly double the area of California. The companies did build, but it was hardly a model of good development: it fueled exploitation of immigrant workers, corruption, speculation, a major financial crisis in 1873, and the rise of the robber barons.

---



**While widely shared abundance** is a worthy aim, it will require a radically different program than further delegating public decision-making to private hands. But Americans do not have to build a program from scratch. They have a useful historical precedent: the New Deal.

Klein and Thompson credit the New Deal for its "boldness" and for cementing the idea that "the federal government must take an active role in managing the American economy and protecting workers." They trace its bipartisan endurance through the Republican administration of Dwight Eisenhower and then briefly chronicle its demise through the administrations of Jimmy Carter, Ronald Reagan, and Bill Clinton. (Though they do not say so, Barack Obama continued this pattern among Democrats.) But remarkably, apart from citing fewer public controls on land use at the time, the book says nothing about why the New Deal was so successful, nor about the populist politics—including Franklin Roosevelt's contempt for "economic royalists"—that undergirded it.

Consider the case of electric modernization—the delivery of abundant, low-cost power to all Americans. In the early 1930s, electricity was common in cities. Most urban households had electricity, though they did not have electricity in the sense we assume today. Working- and middle-class families had lights and a radio, but not the suite of appliances we take for granted today. As historian Ronald Tobey notes, most Americans had electrification, but not electric modernization. But in the countryside, most people did not even have basic electric service. In 1935, only about one in ten farmers had any type of electricity, including generators. A lack of electric service meant candles, no indoor plumbing, storing food in cellars, and doing laundry by hand.

The private sector failed to deliver electric modernization simply because it wasn't profitable. Private electric utilities and their holding company owners wanted quick and easy profits. They discounted the potential for greater residential power consumption and were largely dismissive of the rural market. Private utilities did not want to spend money building lines into thinly populated areas where they believed households, farm and non-farm alike, would not use much power. They instead focused on wealthy households and large industrial customers in cities that used lots of electricity and did not cost much to serve.

**A much more promising path is to embrace a twenty-first-century New Deal—the tried-and-true model for a "liberalism that builds."**

FDR refused to accept this status quo and believed that electric modernization was a necessity. Two months before he was elected in 1932, he presented his vision for the power sector at a campaign stop in Portland, Oregon. He offered a program that was part conservative, part radical: stressing that private ownership should be the norm in electricity, but endorsing much stronger public control over private utilities. Even as he examined the finer points of utility cost accounting, his rhetoric was populist and combative. He condemned holding company "monstrosities" and declared "the public is beginning to understand the need for reform after the same public has been fleeced out of millions of dollars." He further proposed large-scale power generation by federally owned and operated dams on the Colorado, Columbia, Tennessee, and St. Lawrence Rivers—the four corners of the United States. He believed public participation in the power sector could spur the private sector to do better, a philosophy he dubbed "the yardstick."

Soon after taking office, Roosevelt worked with Congress to put the Portland program into practice. In his first 100 days, Congress established the Tennessee Valley Authority (TVA) to build and operate dams on the Tennessee River and its tributaries. The dams would control floods, promote inland navigation, and generate large quantities of low-cost electricity. While Congress ultimately did not create "little TVAs" to cover the rest of the country, it authorized public dam construction across much of the nation.

In the West, the federal Bureau of Reclamation and U.S. Army Corps of Engineers constructed dams like Bonneville and Grand Coulee on the Columbia, Fort Peck on the Missouri, and Shasta on the Sacramento. Private utilities countered that the United States, in the midst of the Great Depression, was already generating excess power, and the dams would only exacerbate the surplus. The mistake was to see consumption as largely fixed, dismissing the possibility that lower rates would stimulate much greater use. In other words, it took public action to break the hold of privately maintained scarcity and deliver abundant power.





To be sure, the national dam building program was hardly perfect. For all the benefits it produced, it carried substantial social and environmental costs—displacing tenant farmers and Native Americans, for example, and decimating fish stocks. But the choices of private actors carry tradeoffs too. The key advantage of Roosevelt's Portland program is that it routed these decisions through public channels. If anything, its negative impacts illustrate the need for more public planning and consultation, not less.

Roosevelt and Congress also launched a major rural electrification program. Created in 1935, the Rural Electrification Administration (REA) offered low-cost credit to build power lines in the countryside. The carrot of cheap financing was not enough to get private utilities off the sidelines. (This experience should counsel against optimism about tax credits and other enticements to clean energy development today.) Instead, the REA turned to a largely untested institutional form—consumer-owned rural electric cooperatives—to build these lines.

The national rural electrification program departed from two prevailing norms today. First, Roosevelt and Congress wanted to bring modern life to the country. They understood people's connections to their communities and sought to bring development to the people, instead of nudging or compelling people to relocate to the comparatively developed cities. Second, rejecting the philosophy that something is better than nothing, the REA called for area service—cooperatives would have to serve all farms and households in their territory, not only the lucrative subset of them. The REA also helped fight "cream skimming" by private utilities, the practice of building lines to serve wealthy farmers and leaving the unprofitable remainder for cooperatives and others.

In line with the Rooseveltian vision of maintaining private ownership and shoring up regulation, Congress strengthened public control of private utilities. In the Public Utility Act of 1935, Congress established regulation of interstate wholesaling and transmission of electricity and broke up and regulated the holding companies that dominated the industry.

The New Deal program was extraordinarily successful. Most visibly, it made rural electrification a reality. Thanks to federal support, the rates of farm electrification skyrocketed in just two decades, rising from one in ten in 1935 to more than nine in ten in 1955. Americans in the countryside got electricity and modern living in the form of indoor plumbing, electric refrigeration, and washing machines that liberated women from the backbreaking work of doing laundry by hand.

Rural cooperatives did the bulk of this line extension, but the private sector stepped up once the federal government showed that rural electrification was a profitable undertaking. The REA arranged a traveling big tent exhibition that showed many uses for electricity on farms and rural homes. It also identified ways of lowering the cost of line construction. Whereas private power had estimated that building rural lines would cost between $1,500 and $2,000 per mile, the REA found that through simplification and standardization of line designs the work could be done for as little as $430 per mile. The public sector led, and the private sector followed and began to recognize the profits to be made in serving rural markets. In line with Roosevelt's own vision, most Americans continued to obtain electricity from private utilities. The New Deal kept private ownership in place but dislodged it from its pride of place.

The New Deal also brought electric modernization to cities. Federal and improved state regulation lowered rates, and public competition helped too. Pressure from federal agencies like TVA as well as a credible threat of public takeovers of utilities—hundreds of cities municipalized their utilities in the '30s—forced private utilities to improve their performance. Public rivalry and stronger public control of private utilities changed their orientation: they exchanged the financial engineering of the 1920s with public service at reasonable profit. Lower rates stimulated greater domestic power consumption. Paired with federal participation in mortgage finance, national power policy brought electric modernization to all.

---

***ABUNDANCE*'S POVERTY OF VISION** does not counsel hopelessness. We have a proven model for achieving broadly shared abundance. The New Deal delivered it through a combination of public investment and stronger public control of private corporations. The state spurred the private sector to adopt a longer-term social orientation in lieu of the extractive governance that had prevailed before the Depression.



That public abundance is still possible. Americans got a small taste of real "supply-side" liberalism in the American Recovery and Reinvestment Act of 2009. Through this program, EPB of Chattanooga, a municipally owned utility created in the 1930s, obtained a federal grant to build a citywide fiber optic network. The utility used these funds to deliver the nation's first 1 gigabyte per second broadband service, helping attract tech companies and workers to the newly dubbed "Gig City."

Replicating this success on a national scale and across a range of urgent challenges calls for a serious revival of New Deal politics, not a doubling down on the ethos of neoliberalism—however appealingly rebranded. **BR**

# CONTRIBUTORS

***Joelle M. Abi-Rached*** is Associate Professor of Medicine at the American University of Beirut and author of *Asfuriyyeh: A History of Madness, Modernity, and War in the Middle East.*

***Samuel Hayim Brody***, Associate Professor of Religious Studies at the University of Kansas, is author of *Martin Buber's Theopolitics.*

***Cathy J. Cohen*** is an activist and D. Gale Johnson Distinguished Service Professor of Political Science at the University of Chicago.

***Vivian Gornick***'s most recent book is *Taking a Long Look: Essays on Culture, Literature, and Feminism in Our Time.*

***Robin D. G. Kelley*** is Distinguished Professor and Gary B. Nash Endowed Chair in U.S. History at UCLA and a contributing editor at *Boston Review*. His many books include *Freedom Dreams: The Black Radical Imagination.*

***Martin O'Neill***, Professor of Political Philosophy at the University of York, is coauthor of *The Case for Community Wealth Building.*

***Elaine Scarry*** is Walter M. Cabot Professor of Aesthetics and General Theory of Value at Harvard University.

***Brandon M. Terry*** is John L. Loeb Associate Professor of the Social Sciences at Harvard University, author of *Shattered Dreams, Infinite Hope: A Tragic Vision of the Civil Rights Movement*, and a member of *Boston Review*'s Board of Advisors.

***Sandeep Vaheesan*** is Legal Director at the Open Markets Institute and author of *Democracy in Power: A History of Electrification in the United States.*

***David Waldstreicher*** is Distinguished Professor of History at the Graduate Center of the City University of New York. His latest book is *The Odyssey of Phillis Wheatley: A Poet's Journeys Through American Slavery and Independence.*

***David Austin Walsh***, a columnist at *Boston Review*, is author of *Taking America Back: The Conservative Movement and the Far Right.*

***Jennifer Zacharia*** is a Palestinian American human rights attorney. She delivered the 2022 Edward Said Memorial Lecture at The Jerusalem Fund.